TAPAS

TAPAS

Authentic appetizers and finger food from the
bars and restaurants of Spain

Pepita Aris

southwater

This edition is published by Southwater

Southwater is an imprint of Anness Publishing Ltd
Hermes House, 88–89 Blackfriars Road, London SE1 8HA
tel. 020 7401 2077; fax 020 7633 9499
www.southwaterbooks.com; info@anness.com

© Anness Publishing Ltd 2005

UK agent: The Manning Partnership Ltd, 6 The Old Dairy,
Melcombe Road, Bath BA2 3LR; tel. 01225 478444;
fax 01225 478440; sales@manning-partnership.co.uk

UK distributor: Grantham Book Services Ltd, Isaac Newton Way,
Alma Park Industrial Estate, Grantham, Lincs NG31 9SD;
tel. 01476 541080; fax 01476 541061; orders@gbs.tbs-ltd.co.uk

North American agent/distributor: National Book Network,
4501 Forbes Boulevard, Suite 200, Lanham, MD 20706;
tel. 301 459 3366; fax 301 429 5746; www.nbnbooks.com

Australian agent/distributor: Pan Macmillan Australia, Level 18,
St Martins Tower, 31 Market St, Sydney, NSW 2000; tel. 1300 135 113;
fax 1300 135 103; customer.service@macmillan.com.au

New Zealand agent/distributor: David Bateman Ltd,
30 Tarndale Grove, Off Bush Road, Albany, Auckland;
tel. (09) 415 7664; fax (09) 415 8892

A CIP catalogue record for this book is available from the British Library.

Publisher: Joanna Lorenz
Editorial Director: Judith Simons
Senior Editors: Susannah Blake and Doreen Gillon
Photographer: Nicki Dowey
Home Economist: Lucy McKelvie
Assistant Home Economist: Emma McKintosh
Stylist: Helen Trent
Designer: Nigel Partridge
Cover Design: Balley Design Associates

Previously published as part of a larger volume, *Spanish Food and Cooking*

1 3 5 7 9 10 8 6 4 2

NOTES

For all recipes, quantities are given in
both metric and imperial measures and,
where appropriate, measures are also
given in standard cups and spoons.
Follow one set, but not a mixture,
because they are not interchangeable.

Standard spoon and cup measures are
level: 1 tsp = 5ml, 1 tbsp = 15ml,
1 cup = 250ml/8fl oz

Australian standard tablespoons are
20ml. Australian readers should use
3 tsp in place of 1 tbsp for measuring
small quantities of gelatine, flour,
salt etc.

Medium (US large) eggs are used
unless otherwise stated.
Bracketed terms are intended
for American readers.

CONTENTS

INTRODUCTION

Tapas are Spain's greatest food invention. "Eat when you drink, drink when you eat" is the philosophy. Spanish men traditionally drink outside the home and rarely alone. Tapas are not meant to be a meal (although a *ración* is a substantial portion). One *tapa* per person and a different one with each drink is the idea, then everyone enjoys tasting and sharing. Tapas food is real food – good local ingredients presented with flair.

The idea comes from Andalusia. It started, so they say, with a piece of bread, soon topped with ham or cheese, balanced over a glass, to keep out the flies – the word *tapa* means a cover. Tapas were once free snacks included in the price of the drink but today they are mostly ordered separately. In dim caverns, where the sherry barrels are stacked high, men revolve the wine in their *copitas*, gently sipping, then select a new wine from a different cask. To compare and contrast is part of the tapas ritual. An old man may sit by the door, with a bucket of *conchas finas*, opening the clams slowly and to order. It is a life less hectic than our own.

Below: An old Seville tapas bar sign advertises food to help sell its drinks.

CLASSIC TAPAS

Tapas dishes revolve around shellfish. In the southern triangle of sherry towns – between Jerez de la Frontera, El Puerto de Santa Maria and Sanlúcar de Barrameda – you may eat amazing shellfish, including squid eggs, whelks (*cañadillas*) and fritters of minute shrimps. The south is also famous for fried fish, *cazón* (a type of shark) marinated in saffron, and *frita malagueña* (mixed battered seafood).

Charcuterie is an important part of the tradition. Hams hang over every bar, with little upturned paper umbrellas underneath to catch dissolving fat: the incomparable scarlet *jamón serrano*.

Above: A row of hams hang behind the bar in a traditional tapas bar in Madrid. This is typical all over Spain.

SOCIAL AMBIENCE

Tapas bars were once the preserve of men. Now they attract women too but they are still a great place to discuss sport, particularly bullfighting. In this macho atmosphere old foods survive, for example squares of blood (set with vinegar) "to give men strength at night". Tapas also fuel Spain's many fiestas. After all, how could one follow an all-night procession without a little bite to eat? A café terrace is also an ideal place from which to watch the spectacle.

Above: A bartender in Madrid pulls a caño, a beer drawn from the pump.

Right: This smart tapas bar in Bilbao, decorated with ornate gilt, entices a sophisticated and loyal clientele.

Pepitas ...

Think "pippy", for *pepitas* are seeds – little nibbles to pick up in handfuls. Toasted chickpeas, soaked *chufas* (tiger nuts), pistachios and large, soaked yellow lupin seeds, *altramuz*. *Pepitas* themselves are creamy-flavoured pumpkin seeds, but also common are *pipas de girasol* (sunflower seeds).

... and pepitos

A *pepito* is a long soft roll (like a bridge roll), often filled with succulent roast veal. A *montadito* (which literally means mounted) is a piece of bread with a topping such as chorizo or (bell) peppers, perhaps speared with a cocktail stick (wooden toothpick). Though the name *bocadillo* translates as mouthful, it is in fact a substantial sandwich of crusty bread, often with ham and cheese.

People go to bars for the company, but stay for the temptations. A range of flavours is offered in tiny portions, from the sophisticated and exotic to the bland and soothing. They are laid out on the counter, like jewels in a shop window: yolk-yellow *tortilla*, kidneys in sherry, red-hot potatoes, Russian salad (*ensaladilla*) and stuffed baby squid.

CITY SPECIALITIES

Madrid favours tripe, *boquerones en vinagre* (fresh anchovy fillets cured in vinegar) and, of course, shellfish. The old tradition was to throw prawn and shrimp heads on the floor of the bar to show how popular the place was. In Barcelona, designer bars are all the rage and people go there to see and be seen. Basque bars in cities reflect a much more bourgeois clientele. The phrase *ir de pinchos* means to go for a tapas crawl, which can be a popular way to spend an evening.

Fried tapas in the north evoke an era of nostalgia, with bechamel-based *croquetas* (croquettes), and *gambas en gabardinas* (prawns/shrimp in batter).

Bars are also the place to find local food specialities such as spider crab in San Sebastián, and elvers and hake throats in Bilbao. The morsels can often be very elaborate: high cuisine presented in miniature. Tapas bars are also a wonderful way to sample Spain's best dishes such as *rabo de toro* (bull's tail) and the delicious *escabeche de perdiz* (vinegared partridge).

TAPAS INGREDIENTS

As well as a variety of vegetables, poultry and meat, there are some typically Spanish ingredients that give tapas their traditional hallmark.

OLIVES

Those olives that are particularly enjoyed as tapas include the very small, greenish-brown *arbequina*, which has a high oil content and pleasant bitter-to-aromatic flavour. It is the Catalan appetizer. The small, round, blue-black *cuquillo* is often prepared with chopped onion and spices and is good served with beer. The largest dark-green, fleshy olives are *gordal* or *reina*, and the most popular type is *manzanilla*, an apple or pear-shaped olive that is suitable for stuffing. *Negra*, which accompanies wine, is a black, dried and pickled olive.

Olive oil

A simple dressing of virgin olive oil brings out the flavour of salads and cooked food. Additionally, olive oil is the best choice for frying as its subtle bitterness counters the rich effects of

Above: Negras perlas *are large, fruity black olives with a mild flavour – perfect as a nibble with a glass of red wine.*

Above: Pimiento-stuffed olives were originally filled by hand.

Left: Manzanillas are the best-known and most popular of Spanish olives.

frying. The high acidity of Spanish oil makes it ideal for making sauces and emulsions, such as *mahonesa* (Spanish mayonnaise), which is perfect with shellfish. *Allioli* – garlic and oil blended to make a thick white sauce – has a stronger flavour, which goes well with vegetables and prawns. The Catalan version includes egg yolk and is served with fish and rice.

Spain's best extra virgin oil (the oil from the first pressing) is clear, golden Nuñez de Prado from Baena. All olive oils should be stored away from direct sunlight and used within three months once opened.

EGGS

Often eaten as everyday meals, eggs also feature in tapas dishes. Perhaps the most well-known is tortilla, where potato, onion and eggs are cooked together until firm and then served in wedges or squares. Frittata is a similar dish, flavoured with herbs and vegetables. Eggs are used in *piperada*, the Basque omelette that includes red and yellow (bell) peppers, and are also delicious softly scrambled with vegetables or shellfish.

Denominación de Origen
As with the system for wine, the best olive-producing areas are given D.O. status, and the quality of their products is carefully regulated.

Left: Olive oil is a key ingredient in so many tapas dishes, from salads and garlicky mayonnaise to marinated and fried foods.

Right: Allioli *is a powerful garlic mayonnaise with a history dating back over 2,000 years.*

Making Mahonesa

Put 2 egg yolks in a bowl with a good pinch of salt. Using a hand-held blender, beat well, then add 30ml/2 tbsp vinegar and beat again. Work in up to 250ml/8fl oz/ 1 cup ordinary (not virgin) olive oil, drizzling very slowly at first, until it becomes thick and creamy. Flavour with lemon juice, extra virgin olive oil and pepper to taste.

FISH

Fried small fish are regularly served in tapas bars, with anchovies and *chanquetes* (whitebait) the most popular. Sardines, however, have an honoured place in Spanish culture, and there are even festivals dedicated to them. They are particularly good as an outdoor food – barbecued or cooked beside the fire on beaches – as are mackerel.

Tuna is highly popular in Spain; the meaty steaks may be fried, grilled (broiled) or cooked on the barbecue. The yellow fin is the most common. It has a darker colour and the meat is less dense than other types of tuna. Swordfish is also regularly eaten and is ideal for grilling. Firm-fleshed monkfish, marinated in herbs, makes excellent kebabs. Of the freshwater fish that grace the tapas table, fresh salmon is the most well-known.

Preserved fish

The Spanish are particularly fond of their preserved fish and the most popular is salt cod, known as *bacalao*. Indeed, whole shops are devoted to it. For tapas dishes strips of salt cod are often simply battered and fried or made into fritters.

Several fish are canned, with tuna especially popular in Spain, where it is served in salads and many other dishes. Indeed, canned white albacore is considered to be tastier than fresh. Sardine canning is a major industry throughout Galicia and the larger sardines are also salted, both in the north and in Huelva. Anchovies are salted as well as canned in oil, when they are called *anchoas*. In the north, some anchovies are brine-pickled before being packed in oil and are often found in the tapas counter. Tiny squid with their ink, and octopus in various sauces, are also canned.

Left: Sardines are popular all over Spain and the freshly caught fish are often cooked on the beach.

Above right: Fine Spanish anchoas are canned in olive oil.

Right: White albacore is the finest type of canned tuna and used

Left: Salt cod, known as bacalao, *is immensely popular and has remained weekly fare in Spain for centuries.*

Below: Canned sardines are widely eaten all over Spain.

Fish caviars

Luxurious caviars are a speciality of the Mediterranean. *Huevas de marucca*, from ling, are among the most common. The best caviar, however, comes from the grey mullet, which thrive in the Murcian salt lagoons in Mar Menor. Other roes available are the golden-brown *huevas de atún* from the blue fin tuna, as well as black herring roe, salmon eggs, and roe from sea bream, hake and anchovy.

SHELLFISH

Tapas dishes often include shellfish, which might be spiced with chilli or cayenne pepper, or flavoured with garlic, wine or sherry They are often fried in olive oil, or it may be simply grilled (broiled) or barbecued.

Galicia is famous for its mussels and scallops, which are often served simply fried. The large and tender mussels are canned as well as sold fresh, and are often breadcrumbed and fried. Clams are common fare, and there are many varieties including the large Venus clam, which measures 8cm/3in across. It is often served with sherry in bars in the south of Spain.

Shrimps and prawns make perfect tapas. Tiny shrimp, called *camarones* have delicate white flesh and make delicious fritters. Other smaller varieties, called *quisquilla*, are added to scrambled eggs and diced vegetable salads. The larger prawns (shrimp), *gamba*, are pink and have a full flavour, which is especially pronounced when battered and fried.

Above: Pressed huevas de marucca *(salted ling roe) is a delicacy but is widely available throughout the country.*

The longest prawns are the excellently flavoured *langostino* and the *carabinero*, which grow to 20cm/8in long and are a deep scarlet colour. Scampi are a luxury and go very well with mayonnaise. Small shore crabs, such as *necoras*, are simply boiled and served whole to be picked and eaten at the table. The strong, sweet flavour of spider crab (*centollo* in Castilian) is a special favourite on the north coast.

Always popular, squid is delicious cut into rings and coated in batter before it is fried as *calamares* (fried squid rings in batter). It is also served in a salad with a mixture of seafood and capers.

Cuttlefish, called *jibia* or *sepia*, and *chocos* and *chiperones* if tiny, are very similar to squid but rounder in shape.

SAUSAGES

There are three types of sausage: black, red and white. *Morcillas*, or black sausages, are blood puddings, which are boiled in cauldrons and then dried, and sometimes smoked. They are almost always cooked again before being eaten. Morcillas are specialities of northern Spain, particularly Extremadura and Asturias. *Morcilla dulce* is eaten raw and often found in tapas bars.

Below: Squid are popularly fried in rings, grilled or stuffed and braised.

Left: Carpetshell clams are very popular and are most often served in sauces.

Right: Gambas are the best of all prawns and have both a wonderful flavour and a lovely texture.

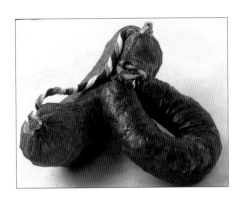

Above: The fat chorizo from Cantimpalo, and the ring-shaped one from Jabugo are two famous versions of this classic spicy paprika sausage.

Paprika is used in sausages across Spain giving them a distinctive red colour, and *choricero chilli* is used for *chorizos*. Cured chorizo is long and fat, and is sliced thinly to eat with bread or cut into little batons and added to salads. *Pamplona* is similar to salami, and *morcon* is made from marinated loin and shoulder, seasoned with paprika. The almost spherical in shape, *sobrasada de Mallorca*, is a smooth pâté-like sausage, which is air-cured for up to a year. *Salchichón* is a "white" sausage served as tapas, and *fuet* is a long and chewy Catalan sausage containing white pepper and sugar.

JAMÓN SERRANO

Serrano means "mountain ham" and is raw and has been dried in cold air. It is long and thin, and triangular at the meaty end. Better ones are marketed

Below: Long, fat cured salchichones *are sliced and served for tapas.*

with the trotter (foot) still attached. Thinly sliced *Serrano* is eaten as tapas or sandwiched with cheese, and it is also used to wrap fish. Little batons are delicious added to salads. Although *jabugo* is probably the Spanish choice for the best ham, *trévelez* is better known abroad.

"White hams" come from the meat of large white pigs, but about 5 per cent of hams are called "black hams" (sold as *ibérico*), which come from the incomparable black native pig, also known as *pata negra* in Spain. The latter are expensive, graded by the food the pigs eat, with *bellota* being the most expensive, made from a pig that has been fed in the wild. Flavoursome *ibérico* ham is cured for 18 months, and then salted for 40–60 days before being matured in the dry winter air. The meat is faintly chewy and varies in colour from deep red to scarlet. The best cuts are from the round side close to the bone.

CHEESE

Although there are many varieties of cheese in Spain only the hard cheeses are usually served as tapas.

The semi-hard *Aragón* and *Gamonedo* cheeses are made with ewe's and goat's milk. Of the purely ewe's milk cheeses, Castile and León produce hard, pressed cheeses with dark rinds, such as *Zamorano D.O.* They are well matured, strong and dense with a grainy texture. Other firm cheeses include *Idiazábal D.O.* from the Basque region, *Grazalema* from Cadiz and *Oduña* from Navarra. Spain's premier cheese is made from the milk of *Manchego* ewes.

Above: Manchego, from left, aged for 4 months, 6 months and 10 months.

Sometimes pasteurized, the curds are heated and then pressed into *esparto* grass moulds.

The cheese is golden inside and gets stronger as it ages. Sold as *semi-curado* (under 13 weeks), *curado* (up to six months) and *viejo* (over six months), and it is also sold packed in oil. The mature (sharp) Manchego cheeses are similar to Parmesan.

BREAD

No Spanish meal is complete without bread. *Mojado* bread is used to scoop up sauced vegetables and seafood tapas, whereas *pa amb tomáquet* is lightly toasted and then topped with olive oil and fresh tomato to start every meal in Catalonia. Slices of bread are used as a base for tapas toppings, such as black pudding, and rolls such as the *bocadillo* are filled with meat, eggs or vegetables. *Torrijas* are bread dipped in milk or wine and then fried and sugared.

Below: Fuet is a chewy, dry sausage from Catalonia.

LIGHT BITES

In Spain, the motto is "eat when you drink, drink when you eat"
— and tapas seem to have been invented for this purpose.
Tapas are finger food, a choice of delicious morsels to tempt
the drinker to have another glass of wine, and with
it another tapas dish.

OLIVE *AND* ANCHOVY BITES

THESE LITTLE MELT-IN-THE-MOUTH MORSELS ARE MADE FROM TWO INGREDIENTS THAT ARE FOREVER ASSOCIATED WITH TAPAS — OLIVES AND ANCHOVIES. THE REASON FOR THIS IS THAT BOTH CONTAIN SALT, WHICH HELPS TO STIMULATE THIRST AND THEREFORE DRINKING.

3 Preheat the oven to 200°C/400°F/ Gas 6. Roll out the dough thinly on a lightly floured surface.

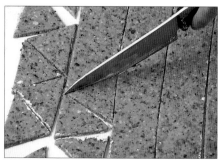

4 Cut the dough into 5cm/2in wide strips, then cut across each strip in alternate directions, to make triangles. Transfer to baking sheets and bake for 8–10 minutes until golden. Cool on a wire rack. Sprinkle with sea salt.

VARIATIONS

• To add a little extra spice, dust the olive and anchovy bites lightly with cayenne pepper before baking.

• Crisp little nibbles set off most drinks. Serve these bites alongside little bowls of seeds and nuts such as sunflower seeds and pistachios. These come in the shell, the opening of which provides a diversion while gossiping. Toasted chickpeas are another popular tapas snack.

MAKES FORTY TO FORTY-FIVE

INGREDIENTS
  115g/4oz/1 cup plain
    (all-purpose) flour
  115g/4oz/½ cup chilled
    butter, diced
  115g/4oz/1 cup finely grated
    Manchego, mature (sharp) Cheddar
    or Gruyère cheese
  50g/2oz can anchovy fillets
    in oil, drained and roughly
    chopped
  50g/2oz/½ cup pitted black olives,
    roughly chopped
  2.5ml/½ tsp cayenne pepper
  sea salt, to serve

1 Place the flour, butter, cheese, anchovies, olives and cayenne pepper in a food processor and pulse until the mixture forms a firm dough.

2 Wrap the dough loosely in clear film (plastic wrap). Chill for 20 minutes.

SWEET AND SALTY VEGETABLE CRISPS

THE SPANISH LOVE NEW AND COLOURFUL SNACKS. TRY THESE BRIGHTLY COLOURED CRISPS, WHICH MAKE AN APPEALING ALTERNATIVE TO POTATO CRISPS. SERVE THEM WITH A BOWL OF CREAMY, GARLICKY ALLIOLI, AND USE THE CRISPS TO SCOOP IT UP.

SERVES FOUR

INGREDIENTS
1 small fresh beetroot (beet)
caster (superfine) sugar and fine salt,
  for sprinkling
olive oil, for frying
coarse sea salt, to serve

COOK'S TIP
Beetroot crisps are particularly flavoursome, but other naturally sweet root vegetables, such as carrots and sweet potato, also taste delicious when cooked in this way. You might like to make several different varieties and serve them heaped in separate small bowls.

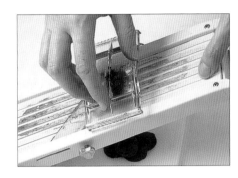

1 Peel the beetroot and, using a mandolin or a vegetable peeler, cut it into very thin slices.

2 Lay the slices on kitchen paper and sprinkle them with sugar and fine salt.

3 Heat 5cm/2in oil in a deep pan until a bread cube turns golden in 1 minute. Cook the slices in batches, until they float to the surface and turn golden at the edge. Drain on kitchen paper and sprinkle with sea salt when cool.

TAPAS OF ALMONDS, OLIVES AND CHEESE

ALMONDS AND OLIVES USED TO BE SERVED FREE IN ALL TAPAS BARS, AND STILL ARE IN SOME. THEY ARE THE PERFECT NIBBLE OR CASUAL STARTER FOR PRE-DINNER DRINKS. MANCHEGO CHEESE IN OIL IS NOW A DELICIOUS SPANISH EXPORT, ALTHOUGH YOU CAN EASILY MARINATE THE CHEESE YOURSELF.

SERVES SIX TO EIGHT

INGREDIENTS
For the marinated olives
  2.5ml/½ tsp coriander seeds
  2.5ml/½ tsp fennel seeds
  2 garlic cloves, crushed
  5ml/1 tsp chopped fresh rosemary
  10ml/2 tsp chopped fresh parsley
  15ml/1 tbsp sherry vinegar
  30ml/2 tbsp olive oil
  115g/4oz/⅔ cup black olives
  115g/4oz/⅔ cup green olives
For the marinated cheese
  150g/5oz Manchego or other
    firm cheese
  90ml/6 tbsp olive oil
  15ml/1 tbsp white wine vinegar
  5ml/1 tsp black peppercorns
  1 garlic clove, sliced
  fresh thyme or tarragon sprigs
  fresh flat leaf parsley or tarragon
    sprigs, to garnish (optional)
For the salted almonds
  1.5ml/¼ tsp cayenne pepper
  30ml/2 tbsp sea salt
  25g/1oz/2 tbsp butter
  60ml/4 tbsp olive oil
  200g/7oz/1¾ cups blanched
    almonds
  extra salt for sprinkling (optional)

1 To make the marinated olives, crush the coriander and fennel seeds in a mortar with a pestle. Work in the garlic, then add the rosemary, parsley, vinegar and olive oil. Put the olives in a small bowl and pour over the marinade. Cover with clear film (plastic wrap) and chill for up to 1 week.

2 To make the marinated cheese, cut the cheese into bitesize pieces, removing any hard rind, and put in a small bowl. Combine the oil, vinegar, peppercorns, garlic, thyme or tarragon and pour over the cheese. Cover with clear film and chill for up to 3 days.

3 To make the salted almonds, combine the cayenne pepper and salt in a bowl. Melt the butter with the oil in a frying pan. Add the almonds and fry them, stirring for 5 minutes, or until golden.

4 Tip the almonds into the salt mixture and toss until the almonds are coated. Leave to cool, then store in an airtight container for up to 1 week.

5 To serve, arrange the almonds, olives and cheese in three separate small, shallow dishes. Garnish the cheese with fresh herbs if you like and scatter the almonds with a little more salt, to taste. Provide cocktail sticks (toothpicks) for guests to pick up the cheese and olives with.

COOK'S TIPS
• Whole olives, sold with the stone, invariably taste better than pitted ones. Don't serve them directly from the brine, but drain and rinse them, then pat dry with kitchen paper. Put the olives in a jar and pour over extra virgin olive oil to cover. Seal and store in the refrigerator for 1–2 months; the flavour of the olives will become enriched. Serve the olives as a tapas dish, or add to salads. When the olives have been eaten, the fruity oil can be used as a dressing for hot food, or made into flavoursome salad dressings.
• A number of exotic stuffed olives are exported from Spain and are widely available in most large supermarkets. Popular varieties include pimiento-stuffed olives, which have been in existence for more than half a century, olives stuffed with salted anchovies, and olives filled with roast garlic.

LITTLE ONIONS COOKED ^{WITH} WINE, CORIANDER ^{AND} OLIVE OIL

CHILLIES AND TOASTED CORIANDER SEEDS ADD PIQUANCY TO THE SMALL ONIONS USED HERE. BAY, GARLIC, THYME, OREGANO, LEMON AND PARSLEY PROVIDE AN UNMISTAKEABLY MEDITERRANEAN KICK.

SERVES SIX

INGREDIENTS
105ml/7 tbsp olive oil
675g/1½lb small onions, peeled
150ml/¼ pint/⅔ cup white wine
2 bay leaves
2 garlic cloves, bruised
1–2 small dried red chillies
15ml/1 tbsp coriander seeds,
  toasted and lightly crushed
2.5ml/½ tsp sugar
a few fresh thyme sprigs
30ml/2 tbsp currants
10ml/2 tsp chopped fresh oregano
5ml/1 tsp grated lemon rind
15ml/1 tbsp chopped fresh flat
  leaf parsley
30–45ml/2–3 tbsp pine nuts, toasted
salt and ground black pepper

1 Place 30ml/2 tbsp olive oil in a wide pan. Add the onions and cook gently over a medium heat for about 5 minutes, or until they begin to colour. Remove from the pan and set aside.

2 Add the remaining oil, the wine, bay leaves, garlic, chillies, coriander, sugar and thyme to the pan. Bring to the boil and cook briskly for 5 minutes. Return the onions to the pan.

COOK'S TIP
You might like to serve this dish as one of several small tapas dishes – perhaps with mustard mayonnaise-dressed celeriac salad and some thinly sliced *jamón serrano* or other air-dried ham and some *fuet* or *chorizo*.

3 Add the currants, reduce the heat and cook gently for 15–20 minutes, or until the onions are soft and tender but not falling apart. Use a draining spoon to transfer the onions to a serving dish.

4 Boil the liquid over a high heat until it reduces considerably. Taste and adjust the seasoning, if necessary, then pour the reduced liquid over the onions. Scatter the oregano over the onions, set aside to cool and then chill them.

5 Just before serving, stir in the grated lemon rind, chopped parsley and toasted pine nuts.

MOJETE

THE SPANISH LOVE TO SCOOP UP COOKED VEGETABLES WITH BREAD, AND THE NAME OF THIS DISH, WHICH IS DERIVED FROM THE WORD MEANING TO DIP, REFLECTS THAT. PEPPERS, TOMATOES AND ONIONS ARE BAKED TOGETHER TO MAKE A COLOURFUL, SOFT VEGETABLE DISH THAT IS STUDDED WITH OLIVES. IN THE SUMMER THE VEGETABLES CAN BE COOKED ON THE BARBECUE.

SERVES EIGHT

INGREDIENTS

2 red (bell) peppers
2 yellow (bell) peppers
1 red onion, sliced
2 garlic cloves, halved
50g/2oz/¼ cup black olives
6 large ripe tomatoes, quartered
5ml/1 tsp soft light brown sugar
45ml/3 tbsp amontillado sherry
3–4 fresh rosemary sprigs
30ml/2 tbsp olive oil
salt and ground black pepper
fresh bread, to serve

1 Halve the peppers and remove the seeds. Cut each pepper lengthways into 12 strips. Preheat the oven to 200°C/400°F/Gas 6.

2 Place the peppers, onion, garlic, olives and tomatoes in a large roasting pan.

3 Sprinkle the vegetables with the sugar, then pour in the sherry. Season well with salt and pepper, cover with foil and bake for 45 minutes.

4 Remove the foil from the pan and stir the mixture well. Add the rosemary sprigs and drizzle with the olive oil. Return the pan to the oven and cook for a further 30 minutes, uncovered, until the vegetables are very tender. Serve hot or cold with plenty of chunks of fresh crusty bread.

COOK'S TIP
Spain is the world's chief olive producer, with half the crop being exported. Try to use good quality Spanish olives for this recipe. Choose unpitted ones as they have a better flavour.

BUÑUELOS

THE NAME OF THESE CHEESE PUFFS LITERALLY MEANS PUFFBALL. IN SPAIN, THEY ARE USUALLY DEEP-FRIED BUT BAKING IS EASIER AND GIVES WONDERFUL RESULTS. THE DOUGH IS MADE IN THE SAME WAY AS FRENCH CHOUX PASTRY, AND THE BUÑUELOS SHOULD BE EATEN WITHIN A FEW HOURS OF BAKING.

SERVES FOUR

INGREDIENTS
  50g/2oz/¼ cup butter, diced
  1.5ml/¼ tsp salt
  250ml/8fl oz/1 cup water
  115g/4oz/1 cup plain
    (all-purpose) flour
  2 whole eggs, plus 1 yolk
  2.5ml/½ tsp Dijon mustard
  2.5ml/½ tsp cayenne pepper
  50g/2oz/½ cup finely grated
    Manchego or Cheddar cheese

1 Preheat the oven to 220°C/425°F/Gas 7. Place butter and the salt in a pan, then add the water. Bring the liquid to the boil. Meanwhile, sift the flour on to a sheet of baking parchment or greaseproof (waxed) paper.

2 Working quickly, tip the flour into the pan of boiling liquid in one go and stir it in immediately.

3 Beat the mixture vigorously with a wooden spoon until it forms a thick paste that binds together and leaves the sides of the pan clean. Remove the pan from the heat.

4 Gradually beat the eggs and yolk into the mixture, then add the mustard, cayenne pepper and cheese.

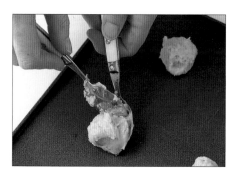

5 Place teaspoonfuls of mixture on a non-stick baking sheet and bake for 10 minutes. Reduce the temperature to 180°C/350°F/Gas 4. Cook for 15 minutes until well browned. Serve hot or cold.

CHICHARRONES

THE SPANISH EAT EVERYTHING THAT COMES FROM THE PIG, AND EVEN THE HUMBLE RIND GOES TO MAKE THIS DELICIOUS LITTLE SALTED, PIQUANT SNACK. THIS CRISPY, CRUNCHY PORK CRACKLING IS THE PERFECT ACCOMPANIMENT FOR A GLASS OF WINE OR CHILLED BOTTLE OF SAN MIGUEL.

SERVES FOUR

INGREDIENTS
  115g/4oz pork rind
  vegetable oil, for frying
  paprika and coarse sea salt,
    for sprinkling

COOK'S TIPS
• Make these cracklings spicier, if you wish. Paprika is the pepper of Spain, and any kitchen may well have one sweet variety (our common paprika), as well as one smoked and one hot – hot chilli powder, cayenne and Tabasco sauce can all be substituted.
• Strips of streaky (fatty) belly can be used instead of pork rind. Cut the strips into the same lengths, removing any bones. Cook them until all the fat has run out, and they look like crisp honeycombs. These tasty morsels are known as *torreznos*.

1 Using a sharp knife, cut the pork rind into strips. There is no need to be too precise, but try to make the strips roughly 1cm/½in wide and 2.5cm/1in long.

2 Pour the vegetable oil to a depth of 2.5cm/1in in a deep heavy frying pan. Heat the oil and check that it has reached the correct temperature by immersing a cube of bread, which should brown in 1 minute.

3 Cook the strips of rind in the oil for 1–2 minutes, until they are puffed up and golden brown. Remove with a slotted spoon and drain on kitchen paper.

4 Sprinkle the chicharrones with paprika and salt to taste. Serve them hot or cold. Although they are at their best 1–2 days after cooking, they will keep reasonably well for up to 2 weeks in an airtight container.

PIMIENTO TARTLETS

Known as tartalitas de pimiento *in* Spain, *these pretty little tartlets are filled with strips of roasted sweet peppers and a deliciously creamy, cheesy custard. They make the perfect snack to serve with drinks.*

SERVES FOUR

INGREDIENTS
  1 red (bell) pepper
  1 yellow (bell) pepper
  175g/6oz/1½ cups plain
   (all-purpose) flour
  75g/3oz/6 tbsp chilled butter, diced
  30–45ml/2–3 tbsp cold water
  60ml/4 tbsp double (heavy) cream
  1 egg
  15ml/1 tbsp grated fresh
   Parmesan cheese
  salt and ground black pepper

VARIATION
Use strips of grilled aubergine (eggplant) mixed with sun-dried tomatoes in place of the roasted peppers.

1 Preheat the oven to 200°C/400°F/ Gas 6, and heat the grill (broiler). Place the peppers on a baking sheet and grill for 10 minutes, turning occasionally, until blackened. Cover with a dishtowel and leave for 5 minutes. Peel away the skin, then discard the seeds and cut the flesh into very thin strips.

2 Sift the flour and a pinch of salt into a bowl. Add the butter and rub it in until the mixture resembles fine breadcrumbs. Stir in enough of the water to make a firm, not sticky, dough.

3 Roll the dough out thinly on a lightly floured surface and line 12 individual moulds or a 12-hole tartlet tin (muffin pan). Prick the bases with a fork and fill the pastry cases with crumpled foil. Bake for 10 minutes.

4 Remove the foil from the pastry cases and divide the pepper strips among the pastry cases.

5 Whisk the cream and egg in a bowl. Season well and pour over the peppers. Sprinkle each tartlet with Parmesan cheese and bake for 15–20 minutes until firm. Cool for 2 minutes, then remove from the moulds and transfer to a wire rack. Serve warm or cold.

SPINACH EMPANADILLAS

LITTLE PIES ARE PART OF THE MOORISH TRADITION IN SPAIN. THE ARABS FIRST BROUGHT SPINACH TO EUROPE AND PINE NUTS AND RAISINS ARE TYPICAL ARAB FLAVOURINGS. IN SPAIN THE DOUGH FOR THESE PASTRIES IS SOLD READY-CUT INTO ROUNDS, AND THEY ARE DEEP-FRIED.

MAKES TWENTY

INGREDIENTS
   25g/1oz/¼ cup raisins
   25ml/1½ tbsp olive oil
   450g/1lb fresh spinach
      leaves, washed, drained
      and chopped
   6 canned anchovies, drained
      and chopped
   2 garlic cloves, finely chopped
   25g/1oz/¼ cup pine nuts,
      roughly chopped
   350g/12oz puff pastry
   1 egg, beaten
   salt and ground black pepper

1 To make the filling, soak the raisins in a little warm water for 10 minutes. Drain well, then chop roughly.

2 Heat the olive oil in a large pan, add the spinach, stir, then cover and cook over a low heat for about 2 minutes until the spinach starts to wilt. Remove the lid, turn up the heat and cook until any liquid has evaporated.

3 Add the chopped anchovies, garlic and seasoning to the spinach and cook, stirring, for about 1 minute.

4 Remove the pan from the heat, then stir in the soaked raisins and pine nuts, and set aside to cool.

5 Meanwhile, preheat the oven to 180°C/350°F/Gas 4. Roll out the pastry on a lightly floured surface to a 3mm/⅛in thickness.

6 Using a 7.5cm/3in pastry cutter, cut the pastry into 20 rounds, re-rolling any scraps if necessary. Place about 10ml/2 tsp filling in the middle of each round, then brush the edges with a little water.

7 Bring up the sides of the pastry and seal well. Press the edges together with the back of a fork. Brush with egg.

8 Place the pies, slightly apart, on a lightly greased baking sheet and bake for about 15 minutes, until puffed up and golden brown.

9 Transfer the pies to a wire rack to cool. They are best served while still slightly warm, but not hot.

VARIATIONS
• Little stuffed pies such as these are typical of Catalonia and the Balearic Islands. Elsewhere in Spain these pies are usually plain, deep-fried and then sugared – the one sweet tapas.
• In the Barcelona food markets, pies filled with a canned tuna and vegetable stuffing are a popular hot snack.

COCA WITH ONION AND ANCHOVY TOPPING

Not unlike Italian pizza, cocas have a very long tradition in Spain. They are essentially fresh bread dough, baked with a variety of savoury toppings, and often include salt fish. The flavourings of this snack go back at least 1000 years.

SERVES SIX TO EIGHT

INGREDIENTS
  400g/14oz/3½ cups strong white
    bread flour
  2.5ml/½ tsp salt
  15g/½oz easy-blend (rapid-rise)
    dried yeast
  120ml/4fl oz/½ cup olive oil
  150ml/¼ pint/⅔ cup milk and water,
    in equal quantities, mixed together
  3 large onions, thinly sliced
  50g/2oz can anchovies, drained and
    roughly chopped
  30ml/2 tbsp pine nuts
  30ml/2 tbsp Muscatel raisins or
    sultanas (golden raisins), soaked
  5ml/1 tsp dried chilli flakes
    or powder
  salt and ground black pepper

VARIATION
You can eat cocas with a wide range of different toppings. Try spinach sautéed with garlic or sweet red (bell) peppers.

1 Put the flour and salt into a food processor with the yeast. Process, gradually working in 60ml/4 tbsp oil and a little of the milk and water. Gradually add the remaining milk and water, processing until well combined. Turn the dough into a bowl, cover with a dishtowel, then leave in a warm place for about 1 hour to rise.

2 Preheat the oven to 240°C/475°F/ Gas 9. Heat the remaining oil in a large frying pan, add the sliced onions, and cook gently until soft.

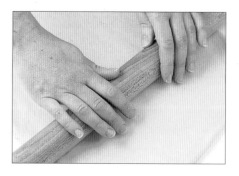

3 Return the dough to the food processor and use the pulse button to work the dough. On a lightly floured surface roll out the dough to a rectangle about 30 × 38cm/12 × 15in. Place on an oiled baking sheet.

4 Cover the dough with the onions. Scatter with the anchovies, pine nuts, raisins or sultanas and chilli flakes or powder and season. Bake for about 10 minutes, until puffed up and the edges are beginning to brown. Serve hot, cut into wedges.

BANDERILLAS

These miniature skewers are very popular in the north of Spain, where they are called pinchos, which literally means stuck on a thorn. Taste, colour and shape guide the choice of ingredients, which may include cold or cured meat, pickled tuna, salted fish or even hard-boiled eggs. In the South, pickled vegetables are preferred. There, the resemblance to the bullfighter's dart was noticed and so the skewers were renamed.

SERVES FOUR

INGREDIENTS
  12 small capers
  12 canned anchovy fillets in
    oil, drained
  12 pitted black olives
  12 cornichons or small gherkins
  12 silverskin pickled onions

VARIATION
You can vary the ingredients if you like, using cold meats, cheeses and vegetables. Choose ingredients with different textures, tastes and colours.

1 Using your fingers, place a caper at the thicker end of each anchovy fillet and carefully roll it up, so that the caper is completely enclosed.

2 Thread one caper-filled anchovy, one olive, one cornichon or gherkin and one pickled onion on to each of 12 cocktail sticks (toothpicks). Chill and serve.

DEEP-FRIED NEW POTATOES WITH SAFFRON ALLIOLI

ALLIOLI IS A SPANISH GARLIC MAYONNAISE, SIMILAR TO THE FRENCH MAYONNAISE OF THE SAME NAME. IN THIS RECIPE SAFFRON ADDS COLOUR AND FLAVOUR.

SERVES FOUR

INGREDIENTS

1 egg yolk
2.5ml/½ tsp Dijon mustard
300ml/½ pint/1¼ cups
   extra virgin olive oil
15–30ml/1–2 tbsp lemon juice
1 garlic clove, crushed
2.5ml/½ tsp saffron threads
20 baby, new or salad potatoes
vegetable oil for frying
salt and ground black pepper

COOK'S TIP
You can also use a food processor or an electric hand whisk to blend the allioli.

1 For the saffron allioli, put the egg yolk in a bowl with the Dijon mustard and a pinch of salt. Stir to mix together well. Beat in the olive oil very slowly, drop by drop at first and then in a very thin stream. Stir in the lemon juice.

2 Season the allioli with salt and ground black pepper then add the crushed garlic and beat into the mixture thoroughly to combine.

3 Place the saffron in a small bowl and add 10ml/2 tsp hot water. Press the saffron with the back of a teaspoon to extract the colour and flavour and leave to infuse for 5 minutes. Beat the saffron and the liquid into the alioli.

4 Cook the potatoes in their skins in boiling salted water for 5 minutes, then turn off the heat. Cover the pan and leave for 15 minutes. Drain the potatoes, then dry them thoroughly in a dish towel.

5 Heat a 1cm/½in layer of vegetable oil in a deep frying pan. When the oil is very hot, add the new potatoes and fry quickly, turning them constantly, until they are crisp and golden all over. Drain on kitchen paper and serve hot with the saffron allioli.

DATES STUFFED WITH CHORIZO AND STREAKY BACON

THIS IS A DELICIOUS SWEET AND SAVOURY COMBINATION FROM SPAIN, USING FRESH SEASONAL DATES, WARM PAPRIKA-FLAVOURED SPICY CHORIZO SAUSAGE.

SERVES FOUR TO SIX

INGREDIENTS
50g/2oz red paprika
   chorizo sausage
12 fresh dates, stoned (pitted)
6 streaky (fatty) bacon
   rashers (strips)
oil, for frying
plain (all-purpose) flour,
   for dusting
1 egg, beaten
50g/2oz/1 cup fresh breadcrumbs

1 Trim the ends of the chorizo sausage and then peel away the skin. Cut into three 2cm/¾in slices. Cut these in half lengthways, then into quarters, making 12 pieces.

2 Stuff each date with a piece of chorizo, closing the date around it. Stretch the bacon, by running the back of a knife along the rasher. Cut each rasher in half, widthways. Wrap a piece of bacon around each date and secure with a wooden cocktail stick.

3 In a deep frying pan, heat 1cm/½in of oil. Dust the dates with flour, dip them in the beaten egg, then coat in breadcrumbs. Fry the dates in the hot oil, turning them, until crisp and golden. Remove the dates with a draining spoon, and drain on kitchen paper. Serve immediately.

FRESH FROM THE SEA

Spain is second only to Japan in fish consumption. There is an abundance of fish tapas and some of the finest fish are caught off the Atlantic coastline. Many exquisite shellfish dishes are to be found along the warm Mediterranean waters.

MARINATED ANCHOVIES

This is one of the simplest ways to prepare these tiny fish because it requires no cooking. Marinating is particularly associated with anchovies, which tend to lose their freshness very quickly. The Spanish term for marinated anchovies is boquerones, *while* anchoas *is the word for the canned, salted variety.*

2 Using the tip of a small, sharp knife, carefully remove the backbones from the flattened fish, and arrange the anchovies skin side down in a single layer on a large plate.

3 Squeeze two-thirds of the lemon juice over the fish and sprinkle them with the salt. Cover and leave to stand for 1–24 hours, basting occasionally with the juices, until the flesh is white and no longer translucent.

4 Transfer the anchovies to a serving plate and drizzle with the olive oil and the remaining lemon juice. Scatter the fish with the chopped garlic and parsley, then cover with clear film (plastic wrap) and chill until ready to serve.

SERVES FOUR

INGREDIENTS
225g/8oz fresh anchovies, heads
    and tails removed, and split open
    along the belly
juice of 3 lemons
30ml/2 tbsp extra virgin olive oil
2 garlic cloves, finely chopped
15ml/1 tbsp chopped fresh parsley
flaked sea salt

1 Turn the anchovies on to their bellies, and press down with your thumb.

THREE-COLOURED FISH KEBABS

BROCHETAS AND PINCHOS ARE POPULAR ALL OVER SPAIN. THIS DELICIOUS RECIPE USES FISH WITH A MEATIER TEXTURE, WHICH IS IDEAL FOR BARBECUES AND GRILLS. DON'T LEAVE THE FISH TO MARINATE FOR MORE THAN AN HOUR. THE LEMON JUICE WILL START TO BREAK DOWN THE FIBRES OF THE FISH AFTER THIS TIME AND IT WILL THEN BE DIFFICULT TO AVOID OVERCOOKING IT.

SERVES FOUR

INGREDIENTS
  120ml/4fl oz/½ cup extra virgin
    olive oil
  finely grated rind and juice of
    1 large lemon
  5ml/1 tsp crushed chilli flakes
  350g/12oz monkfish fillet, cubed
  350g/12oz swordfish fillet, cubed
  350g/12oz thick salmon fillet or
    steak, cubed
  2 red, yellow or orange (bell)
    peppers, cored, seeded and cut
    into squares
  30ml/2 tbsp finely chopped
    fresh flat leaf parsley
  salt and ground black pepper

FOR THE SWEET TOMATO AND
CHILLI SALSA
  225g/8oz ripe tomatoes,
    finely chopped
  1 garlic clove, crushed
  1 fresh red chilli, seeded
    and chopped
  45ml/3 tbsp extra virgin
    olive oil
  15ml/1 tbsp lemon juice
  15ml/1 tbsp finely chopped fresh
    flat leaf parsley
  pinch of sugar

1 Put the extra virgin olive oil in a shallow glass or china bowl and add the lemon rind and juice, the crushed chilli flakes and pepper to taste. Whisk to combine, then add the fish chunks. Turn to coat the fish evenly. Preheat the barbecue or grill (broiler).

VARIATIONS
• Use tuna fish steaks (*atún*) instead of swordfish (*pez espada*), if you like. It has a similar meaty texture, is highly nutritious and will be equally successful in this recipe.
• Dogfish (*cazón*) and sharks such as *cailón* (porbeagle/mackerel shark) are also good marinated and grilled.

2 Add the pepper squares, stir, then cover and marinate in a cool place for 1 hour, turning occasionally with a slotted spoon.

3 Thread the fish and peppers on to eight oiled metal skewers, reserving the marinade. Cook the skewered fish on the barbecue or under the grill for 5–8 minutes, turning once.

4 Meanwhile, make the salsa by mixing all the ingredients in a bowl, and seasoning to taste with salt and pepper. Heat the reserved marinade in a small pan, remove from the heat and stir in the parsley, with salt and pepper to taste. Serve the kebabs hot, with the marinade spooned over, accompanied by the salsa.

SALT COD FRITTERS WITH ALLIOLI

BACALAO — SALT COD — IS ONE OF THE GREAT SPANISH DELIGHTS, ADDING FLAVOUR TO BLAND INGREDIENTS SUCH AS POTATOES. IF YOU ARE UNFAMILIAR WITH IT, THEN THIS IS A DELIGHTFUL WAY TO TRY IT OUT. BITESIZE FISH CAKES, DIPPED INTO RICH, CREAMY, GARLICKY ALLIOLI, ARE IRRESISTIBLE AS A TAPAS DISH OR APPETIZER.

SERVES SIX

INGREDIENTS
   450g/1lb salt cod
   500g/1¼lb floury potatoes
   300ml/½ pint/1¼ cups milk
   6 spring onions (scallions),
      finely chopped
   30ml/2 tbsp extra virgin olive oil
   30ml/2 tbsp chopped fresh parsley
   juice of ½ lemon
   2 eggs, beaten
   plain (all-purpose) flour, for dusting
   90g/3½oz/1¼ cups dried white
      breadcrumbs
   olive oil, for shallow frying
   lemon wedges and salad leaves,
      to serve
   salt and ground black pepper
For the allioli
   2 large garlic cloves, finely chopped
   2 egg yolks
   300ml/½ pint/1¼ cups olive oil
   juice of ½ lemon, to taste

1 Soak the salt cod in cold water for at least 24 hours, changing the water two or three times. The cod should swell as it rehydrates. Sample a tiny piece. It should not taste unpleasantly salty when fully rehydrated. Drain well and pat dry with kitchen paper.

2 Cook the potatoes, unpeeled, in a pan of lightly salted boiling water for about 20 minutes, until tender. Drain. As soon as they are cool enough to handle, peel the potatoes, then mash with a fork or use a potato masher.

3 Pour the milk into a pan, add half the spring onions and bring to a simmer. Add the soaked cod and poach very gently for 10–15 minutes, or until it flakes easily. Remove the cod and flake it with a fork into a bowl, discarding bones and skin.

4 Add 60ml/4 tbsp mashed potato to the cod and beat them together with a wooden spoon. Work in the olive oil, then gradually add the remaining mashed potato. Beat in the remaining spring onions and the parsley.

5 Season with lemon juice and pepper to taste – the mixture may also need a little salt but taste it before adding any. Add one egg to the mixture and beat in until thoroughly combined, then chill until firm.

6 Shape the chilled fish mixture into 12–18 balls, then gently flatten into small round cakes. Coat each one in flour, then dip in the remaining beaten egg and coat with dried breadcrumbs. Chill until ready to fry.

7 Meanwhile, make the allioli. Place the garlic and a good pinch of salt in a mortar and pound to a paste with a pestle. Using a small whisk or a wooden spoon, gradually work in the egg yolks.

8 Beat in about half the olive oil, a drop at a time. When the sauce is as thick as soft butter, beat in 5–10ml/1–2 tsp lemon juice. Continue adding oil until the allioli is very thick. Season to taste, adding more lemon juice if you wish.

9 Heat about 2cm/¾in oil in a large, heavy frying pan. Add the fritters and cook over a medium-high heat for about 4 minutes. Turn them over and cook for a further 4 minutes on the other side, until crisp and golden. Drain on kitchen paper, then serve with the allioli, lemon wedges and salad leaves.

COOK'S TIP
Try to find a thick, creamy white piece of salt cod, preferably cut from the middle of the fish rather than the tail and fin ends. Avoid thin, yellowish salt cod, as it will be too dry and salty.

CEVICHE

You can use almost any firm-fleshed fish for this Spanish influenced dish, provided that it is perfectly fresh. The fish is "cooked" by the action of the acidic lime juice. Adjust the amount of chilli according to your taste.

SERVES SIX

INGREDIENTS
    675g/1½lb halibut, turbot, sea bass
      or salmon fillets, skinned
    juice of 3 limes
    1–2 fresh red chillies, seeded and
      very finely chopped
    15ml/1 tbsp olive oil
    salt
For the garnish
    4 large firm tomatoes, peeled,
      seeded and diced
    1 ripe avocado, peeled
      and diced
    15ml/1 tbsp lemon juice
    30ml/2 tbsp olive oil
    30ml/2 tbsp fresh coriander
      (cilantro) leaves

1 Cut the fish into strips measuring about 5 × 1cm/2 × ½ in. Lay these in a shallow dish and pour over the lime juice, turning the fish strips to coat them all over in the juice. Cover with clear film (plastic wrap) and leave for 1 hour.

2 Mix all the garnish ingredients, except the coriander, together. Set aside.

3 Season the fish with salt and scatter over the chillies. Drizzle with the oil. Toss the fish in the mixture, then replace the cover. Leave to marinate in the refrigerator for 15–30 minutes more.

4 To serve, divide the garnish among six plates. Spoon on the ceviche, sprinkle with coriander and serve.

SURTIDO DE PESCADO

THE SPANISH ENJOY AND MAKE THE MOST OF PRESERVED FISH. THIS IS A VERY PRETTY DISH, WHICH USES WHATEVER IS EASILY AVAILABLE, AND IT MAKES AN IDEAL LAST-MINUTE PARTY APPETIZER. FOR THE BEST RESULTS TRY TO USE SPANISH CANNED FISH.

SERVES FOUR

INGREDIENTS

6 eggs
cos or romaine lettuce leaves
75–90ml/5–6 tbsp mayonnaise
90g/3½oz jar Avruga herring roe,
   Eurocaviar grey mullet roe or
   undyed (or black) lumpfish roe
2 × 115g/4oz cans sardines
   in oil
2 × 115g/4oz cans mackerel
   fillets in oil
2 × 150g/5oz jars cockles (small
   clams) in brine, drained
2 × 115g/4oz cans mussels
   or scallops in tomato sauce
fresh flat leaf parsley or dill sprigs,
   to garnish

COOK'S TIP

Smoked salmon, kippers (smoked herrings) and rollmops (pickled herring fillets) can also be included on the platter. Try to maintain a balance between fish or shellfish pickled in brine or vinegar, with those in oil or sauce. Huge Spanish mussels *en escabeche* (spicy sauce) are now available in large supermarkets. Also look out for Spanish fish roes to top the eggs.

1 Put the eggs in a pan with enough water to cover and bring to the boil. Turn down the heat and simmer for 10 minutes. Drain immediately, then cover with cold water and set aside until completely cool. Peel the eggs and slice in half.

2 Arrange the lettuce leaves on a large serving platter, with the tips pointing outwards. (You may need to break off the bottom end of each leaf if the leaves are large).

3 Place a teaspoonful or so of mayonnaise on the flat side of each halved egg and top with a spoonful of fish caviar. Carefully arrange in the centre of the dish.

4 Arrange the sardines and mackerel fillets at four points on the plate. Spoon the pickled cockles into two of the gaps, opposite each other, and the mussels in sauce in the remaining gaps. Garnish with parsley sprigs or dill. Place in the refrigerator until needed.

FRIED WHITEBAIT WITH SHERRY SALSA

SMALL FRESHLY FRIED FISH ARE OFFERED IN EVERY TAPAS BAR IN SPAIN. BLACK-BACKED ANCHOVIES ARE THE BEST, BUT NEED TO BE COOKED WITHIN A DAY OF CATCHING. TINY CHANQUETES ARE ALSO GOOD, BUT ANY SMALL FISH, SUCH AS WHITEBAIT, ARE SUITABLE. SERVE THEM WITH LEMON WEDGES.

SERVES FOUR

INGREDIENTS

225g/8oz whitebait
30ml/2 tbsp seasoned plain (all-purpose) flour
60ml/4 tbsp olive oil
60ml/4 tbsp sunflower oil

For the salsa

1 shallot, finely chopped
2 garlic cloves, finely chopped
4 ripe tomatoes, roughly chopped
1 small red chilli, seeded and finely chopped
30ml/2 tbsp olive oil
60ml/4 tbsp sweet oloroso sherry
30–45ml/2–3 tbsp chopped mixed fresh herbs, such as parsley or basil
25g/1oz/½ cup stale white breadcrumbs
salt and ground black pepper

1 To make the salsa, place the chopped shallot, garlic, tomatoes, chilli and olive oil in a pan. Cover with a lid and cook gently for about 10 minutes.

2 Pour the sherry into the pan and season with salt and pepper to taste. Stir in the herbs and breadcrumbs, then cover and keep the salsa hot until the whitebait are ready.

3 Preheat the oven to 150°C/300°F/ Gas 2. Wash the whitebait thoroughly, drain well and dry on kitchen paper, then dust in the seasoned flour.

4 Heat the oils together in a heavy frying pan and cook the fish in batches until crisp and golden. Drain on kitchen paper and keep warm until all the fish are cooked. Serve at once with the salsa.

ENSALADA DE MARISCOS

YOU CAN VARY THE SEAFOOD IN THIS TASTY SALAD ACCORDING TO WHAT IS AVAILABLE, BUT TRY TO INCLUDE AT LEAST TWO KINDS OF SHELLFISH AND SOME SQUID. THE SALAD IS GOOD WARM OR COLD.

SERVES SIX AS AN APPETIZER,
FOUR AS A MAIN COURSE

INGREDIENTS
  450g/1lb live mussels, scrubbed
    and bearded
  450g/1lb small clams, scrubbed
  105ml/7 tbsp dry white wine
  225g/8oz squid, cleaned
  4 large scallops, with their corals
  30ml/2 tbsp olive oil
  2 garlic cloves, finely chopped
  1 small dried red chilli, crumbled
  225g/8oz whole cooked prawns
    (shrimp), in the shell
  6–8 large chicory (endive) leaves
  6–8 radicchio leaves
  15ml/1 tbsp chopped flat leaf
    parsley, to garnish
For the dressing
  5ml/1 tsp Dijon mustard
  30ml/2 tbsp white wine or
    cider vinegar
  5ml/1 tsp lemon juice
  120ml/4fl oz/½ cup extra virgin
    olive oil
  salt and ground black pepper

1 Put the mussels and clams in a large pan with the white wine. Cover and cook over a high heat, shaking the pan occasionally, for about 4 minutes, until they have opened. Discard any that remain closed. Use a slotted spoon to transfer the shellfish to a bowl, then strain and reserve the cooking liquid and set it aside.

2 Cut the squid into thin rings; chop the tentacles. Leave small squid whole. Halve the scallops horizontally.

3 Heat the oil in a frying pan, add the garlic, chilli, squid, scallops and corals, and sauté for about 2 minutes, until just cooked and tender. Lift the squid and scallops out of the pan; reserve the oil.

4 When the shellfish are cool enough to handle, shell them, keeping a dozen of each in the shell. Peel all but 6–8 of the prawns. Pour the shellfish cooking liquid into a small pan, set over a high heat and reduce by half. Mix all the shelled and unshelled mussels and clams with the squid and scallops, then add the prawns.

5 To make the dressing, whisk the mustard with the vinegar and lemon juice and season to taste. Add the olive oil, whisk vigorously, then whisk in the reserved cooking liquid and the oil from the frying pan. Pour the dressing over the seafood mixture and toss lightly to coat well.

6 Arrange the chicory and radicchio leaves around the edge of a large serving dish and pile the mixed seafood salad into the centre. Sprinkle with the chopped flat leaf parsley and serve immediately or chill first.

KING PRAWNS IN CRISPY BATTER

A HUGE RANGE OF PRAWNS IS ENJOYED IN SPAIN, EACH WITH ITS APPROPRIATE COOKING METHOD. LANGOSTINOS ARE DEEP-WATER PRAWNS, OFTEN WITH TIGER STRIPES, AND CAN BE AMONG THE BIGGEST. THE BEST WAY TO ENJOY THEM IS DIPPED IN A SIMPLE BATTER AND DEEP-FRIED.

SERVES FOUR

INGREDIENTS
  120ml/4fl oz/½ cup water
  1 large (US extra large) egg
  115g/4oz/1 cup plain
    (all-purpose) flour
  5ml/1 tsp cayenne pepper
  12 raw king prawns (jumbo shrimp),
    in the shell
  vegetable oil, for deep frying
  flat leaf parsley, to garnish
  lemon wedges, to serve (optional)

COOK'S TIP
Leaving the tails on the prawns makes them easier to pick up and eat, and also look very pretty once cooked.

1 In a large bowl, whisk together the water and the egg. Whisk in the flour and cayenne pepper until smooth.

2 Peel the prawns, leaving just the tails intact. Make a shallow cut down the back of each prawn.

3 Using the tip of the knife, pull out and discard the dark intestinal tract.

4 Heat the oil in a large pan or deep-fat fryer, until a cube of bread dropped into the oil browns in 1 minute.

5 Holding the prawns by their tails, dip them into the batter, one at a time, shaking off any excess. Carefully drop each prawn into the oil and fry for 2–3 minutes until crisp and golden. Drain on kitchen paper, garnish with parsley and serve with lemon wedges, if you like.

VARIATION
If you have any batter left over, use it to coat thin strips of vegetables such as sweet potato, beetroot (beet), carrot or (bell) pepper, or use small broccoli florets or whole baby spinach leaves. Deep-fry the vegetables until golden.

BUTTERFLIED PRAWNS IN CHOCOLATE SAUCE

THERE IS A LONG TRADITION IN SPAIN, WHICH ORIGINATES IN MEXICO, OF COOKING SAVOURY FOOD — EVEN SHELLFISH — WITH CHOCOLATE. KNOWN AS LANGOSTINOS EN CHOCOLATE IN SPANISH, THIS IS JUST THE KIND OF CULINARY ADVENTURE THAT BASQUE CHEFS LOVE.

SERVES FOUR

INGREDIENTS

- 8 large raw prawns (shrimp), in the shell
- 15ml/1 tbsp seasoned plain (all-purpose) flour
- 15ml/1 tbsp pale dry sherry
- juice of 1 large orange
- 15g/½oz dark (bittersweet) chocolate, chopped
- 30ml/2 tbsp olive oil
- 2 garlic cloves, finely chopped
- 2.5cm/1in piece fresh root ginger, finely chopped
- 1 small dried chilli, seeded and chopped
- salt and ground black pepper

1 Peel the prawns, leaving just the tail sections intact. Make a shallow cut down the back of each one and carefully pull out and discard the dark intestinal tract.

2 Turn the prawns over so that the undersides are uppermost, and then carefully slit them open from tail to top, using a small sharp knife, cutting them almost, but not quite, through to the central back line.

3 Press the prawns down firmly to flatten them out. Coat with the seasoned flour and set aside.

4 Gently heat the sherry and orange juice in a small pan. When warm, remove from the heat and stir in the chopped chocolate until melted.

5 Heat the oil in a frying pan. Add the garlic, ginger and chilli and cook for 2 minutes until golden. Remove with a slotted spoon and reserve. Add the prawns, cut side down and cook for 2–3 minutes until golden brown with pink edges. Turn the prawns and cook for a further 2 minutes.

6 Return the garlic mixture to the pan and pour the chocolate sauce over. Cook for 1 minute, turning the prawns to coat them in the glossy sauce. Season to taste and serve hot.

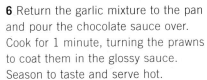

Sizzling Garlic Prawns

Garlic prawns are hugely popular in Spain, both with and without the addition of chilli. They are normally cooked in small, individual earthenware casseroles, which stand on an iron baking sheet — la plancha. A frying pan will produce the same result.

SERVES FOUR

INGREDIENTS
  1–2 dried chillies (to taste)
  60ml/4 tbsp olive oil
  3 garlic cloves, finely chopped
  16 large raw prawns (shrimp),
   in the shell
  salt and ground black pepper
  French bread, to serve

VARIATION
To make classic *gambas al ajillo* – garlic prawns (shrimp) – simply omit the chilli. The word *ajillo* tells you how the garlic is prepared. The diminutive means finely chopped, like the garlic in the final dish. The alternative is *gambas con ajo*, which means with garlic. For this dish, slices of garlic are fried until brown, to flavour the oil, then discarded.

1 Split the chillies lengthways and discard the seeds. It is best to do this with a knife and fork, because the seeds, in particular, contain hot capsicum, which can be very irritating to the eyes, nose and mouth.

2 Heat the oil in a large frying pan and stir-fry the garlic and chilli for 1 minute, until the garlic begins to turn brown.

3 Add the whole prawns and stir-fry for 3–4 minutes, coating them well with the flavoured oil.

4 Remove from the heat and divide the prawns among four dishes. Spoon over the flavoured oil and serve immediately. (Remember to provide a plate for the heads and shells, plus plenty of napkins for messy fingers.)

SPICED CLAMS

SPANISH CLAMS, ESPECIALLY IN THE NORTH, ARE MUCH LARGER THAN CLAMS FOUND ELSEWHERE, AND HAVE MORE SUCCULENT BODIES. THIS MODERN RECIPE USES ARAB SPICING TO MAKE A HOT DIP OR SAUCE. SERVE WITH PLENTY OF FRESH BREAD TO MOP UP THE DELICIOUS JUICES.

SERVES THREE TO FOUR

INGREDIENTS

1 small onion, finely chopped
1 celery stick, sliced
2 garlic cloves, finely chopped
2.5cm/1in piece fresh root
  ginger, grated
30ml/2 tbsp olive oil
1.5ml/¼ tsp chilli powder
5ml/1 tsp ground turmeric
30ml/2 tbsp chopped
  fresh parsley
500g/1¼lb small clams, in
  the shell
30ml/2 tbsp dry white wine
salt and ground black pepper
celery leaves, to garnish
fresh bread, to serve

COOK'S TIPS
• There are many different varieties of clam fished off the coast of Spain. One of the best is the *almeja fina* (the carpet shell clam), which is perfect used in this dish. They have grooved brown shells with a yellow lattice pattern.
• Before cooking the clams, check that all the shells are closed. Any clams that do not open after cooking should be discarded.

1 Place the onion, celery, garlic and ginger in a large pan, add the olive oil, spices and chopped parsley and stir-fry for about 5 minutes. Add the clams to the pan and cook for 2 minutes.

2 Add the wine, then cover and cook gently for 2–3 minutes, shaking the pan occasionally. Season. Discard any clams whose shells remain closed, then serve, garnished with the celery leaves.

MUSSELS <u>WITH A</u> PARSLEY CRUST

THE STORMY ATLANTIC COAST OF SPAIN PRODUCES THE BEST MUSSELS IN THE WORLD. KNOWN AS MEJILLONES IN SPAIN, THEY GROW TO ENORMOUS SIZE IN A VERY SHORT TIME, WITHOUT BECOMING TOUGH. HERE THEY ARE GRILLED WITH A DELICIOUSLY FRAGRANT TOPPING OF PARMESAN CHEESE, GARLIC AND PARSLEY, WHICH HELPS TO PREVENT THE MUSSELS FROM BECOMING OVERCOOKED.

SERVES FOUR

INGREDIENTS
   450g/1lb fresh mussels
   45ml/3 tbsp water
   15ml/1 tbsp melted butter
   15ml/1 tbsp olive oil
   45ml/3 tbsp freshly grated
     Parmesan cheese
   30ml/2 tbsp chopped fresh parsley
   2 garlic cloves, finely chopped
   2.5ml/½ tsp coarsely ground
     black pepper
   crusty bread, to serve

COOK'S TIP
Steaming the mussels produces about 250ml/8fl oz/1 cup wonderful shellfish stock that can be used in other fish and shellfish recipes. Once the mussels have been steamed, remove them from the pan and leave the broth liquor to cool, then store it in a sealed container in the refrigerator or freezer.

Combining fish and shellfish stock is the backbone of many Spanish fish dishes such as *merluza con salsa verde* (hake with green sauce). It is said that the stock from one shellfish makes the best sauce for another.

1 Scrub the mussels thoroughly, scraping off any barnacles with a round-bladed knife and pulling out the gritty beards. Sharply tap any open mussels and discard any that fail to close or whose shells are broken.

2 Place the mussels in a large pan and add the water. Cover the pan with a lid and steam for about 5 minutes, or until the mussel shells have opened.

3 Drain the mussels well and discard any that remain closed. Carefully snap off the top shell from each mussel, leaving the actual flesh still attached to the bottom shell.

4 Balance the shells in a flameproof dish, packing them closely together to make sure that they stay level.

5 Preheat the grill (broiler) to high. Put the melted butter, olive oil, grated Parmesan cheese, parsley, garlic and black pepper in a small bowl and mix well to combine.

6 Spoon a small amount of the cheese and garlic mixture on top of each mussel and gently press down with the back of the spoon.

7 Grill (broil) the mussels for about 2 minutes, or until they are sizzling and golden. Serve the mussels in their shells, with plenty of bread to mop up the delicious juices.

COOK'S TIP
Give each guest one of the discarded top shells of the mussels. They can be used as a little spoon to free the body from the shell of the next. Scoop up the mussel in the empty shell and tip the shellfish and topping into your mouth.

GRATIN OF MUSSELS WITH PESTO

THIS IS THE PERFECT APPETIZER FOR SERVING WHEN TIME IS SHORT, AS BOTH THE PESTO AND THE MUSSELS CAN BE PREPARED IN ADVANCE, AND THE DISH ASSEMBLED AND GRILLED AT THE LAST MINUTE.

SERVES FOUR

INGREDIENTS
36 large live mussels, scrubbed
   and bearded
105ml/7 tbsp dry white wine
60ml/4 tbsp finely chopped fresh
   flat leaf parsley
1 garlic clove, finely chopped
30ml/2 tbsp fresh white breadcrumbs
60ml/4 tbsp olive oil
chopped fresh basil, to garnish
crusty bread, to serve
For the pesto
2 fat garlic cloves, chopped
2.5ml/½ tsp coarse salt
100g/3¾ oz/3 cups basil leaves
25g/1oz/⅓ cup pine nuts, chopped
50g/2oz/⅔ cup freshly grated
   Parmesan cheese
120ml/4fl oz/½ cup extra virgin
   olive oil

1 Put the mussels in a pan with the wine, clamp on the lid and shake over high heat for 3–4 minutes until the mussels have opened. Discard any which remain closed.

2 As soon as the mussels are cool enough to handle, strain the cooking liquid and keep it for another recipe. Discard the empty half-shells. Arrange the mussels in their half-shells in a single layer in four individual gratin dishes. Cover and set aside.

COOK'S TIP
Home-made pesto is best but when basil is out of season – or you are in a hurry – a jar may be used instead.

3 To make the pesto, put the chopped garlic and salt in a mortar and pound to a purée with a pestle. Then add the basil leaves and chopped pine nuts and crush to a thick paste. Work in the Parmesan cheese, and finally gradually drip in enough olive oil to make a smooth and creamy paste. Alternatively, use a food processor.

4 Spoon pesto over the mussels placed in gratin dishes. Mix the parsley, garlic and breadcrumbs. Sprinkle over the mussels. Drizzle with the oil.

5 Preheat the grill (broiler) to high. Stand the dishes on a baking sheet and grill for 3 minutes. Garnish with chopped basil and serve with crusty bread.

POTATO, MUSSEL <u>AND</u> WATERCRESS SALAD

*THE MUSSELS FOUND ON THE GALICIAN COAST ARE THE BEST IN THE WORLD. THE GALICIANS ARE
ALSO VERY PROUD OF THEIR POTATOES AND THEIR WATERCRESS. IN ENSALADA DE MEJILLONES,
PATATAS Y BERROS A CREAMY, WELL-FLAVOURED DRESSING ENHANCES ALL THESE INGREDIENTS.*

SERVES FOUR

INGREDIENTS
675g/1½lb salad potatoes
1kg/2¼lb mussels, scrubbed
and beards removed
200ml/7fl oz/scant 1 cup dry
white wine
15g/½oz fresh flat leaf
parsley, chopped
1 bunch of watercress
or rocket (arugula)
salt and ground black pepper
chopped fresh chives or
spring onion (scallion) tops,
to garnish
For the dressing
105ml/7 tbsp olive oil
15–30ml/1–2 tbsp white wine vinegar
5ml/1 tsp strong Dijon mustard
1 large shallot, very finely chopped
15ml/1 tbsp chopped fresh chives
45ml/3 tbsp double (heavy) cream
pinch of caster (superfine)
sugar (optional)

1 Cook the potatoes in salted boiling
water for 15–20 minutes, or until
tender. Drain, cool, then peel. Slice the
potatoes into a bowl and toss with
30ml/2 tbsp of the oil for the dressing.

2 Discard any open mussels. Bring the
white wine to the boil in a large, heavy
pan. Add the mussels, cover and boil
vigorously, shaking the pan occasionally,
for 3–4 minutes, until the mussels have
opened. Discard any that do not open.
Drain and shell the mussels, reserving
the cooking liquid.

3 Boil the reserved mussel cooking
liquid until reduced to about 45ml/
3 tbsp. Strain this through a fine sieve
over the potatoes and toss to mix.

4 Make the dressing. Whisk together the
remaining oil, 15ml/1 tbsp of the
vinegar, the mustard, shallot and chives.

5 Add the cream and whisk again
to form a thick dressing. Adjust the
seasoning, adding more vinegar and/
or a pinch of sugar to taste.

6 Toss the mussels with the potatoes,
then gently mix in the dressing and
chopped parsley. Arrange the
watercress or rocket on a serving platter
and top with the salad. Serve sprinkled
with extra chives or a little spring onion.

COOK'S TIP
Potato salads such as this one should
not be chilled if at all possible because
chilling alters the texture of the
potatoes. For the best flavour and
texture, serve this salad just cool or at
room temperature.

SEAFOOD SALAD

THIS IS A VERY PRETTY ARRANGEMENT OF FRESH MUSSELS, PRAWNS AND SQUID RINGS SERVED ON A COLOURFUL BED OF SALAD VEGETABLES. IN SPAIN, CANNED ALBACORE TUNA IS ALSO OFTEN INCLUDED IN THIS TYPE OF SIMPLE FISH SALAD.

2 Discard any open mussels that do not close when tapped. Cover the base of a large pan with water, add the mussels, then cover and steam for a few minutes until they open. Discard any that remain shut.

3 Using a swivel-style vegetable peeler, cut the carrot into wafer-thin ribbons. Tear the lettuce into pieces and arrange on a serving plate. Scatter the carrot ribbons on top, then sprinkle over the diced cucumber.

4 Arrange the mussels, prawns and squid rings over the salad and scatter the capers over the top.

5 Make the dressing. Put all the ingredients in a small bowl and whisk well to combine. Drizzle over the salad. Serve at room temperature.

SERVES SIX

INGREDIENTS
    115g/4oz prepared squid rings
    12 fresh mussels, scrubbed and
      beards removed
    1 large carrot
    6 crisp lettuce leaves
    10cm/4in piece cucumber,
      finely diced
    115g/4oz cooked, peeled
      prawns (shrimp)
    15ml/1 tbsp drained pickled capers
For the dressing
    30ml/2 tbsp freshly squeezed
      lemon juice
    45ml/3 tbsp virgin olive oil
    15ml/1 tbsp chopped fresh parsley
    salt and ground black pepper

1 Put the squid rings into a metal sieve or vegetable steamer. Place the sieve or steamer over a pan of simmering water, cover with a lid and steam the squid for 2–3 minutes until it just turns white. Cool under cold running water to prevent further cooking and drain thoroughly on kitchen paper.

VIEIRAS DE SANTIAGO

SCALLOPS ARE THE SYMBOL OF ST JAMES (SANTIAGO), AND THIS DISH IS ASSOCIATED WITH HIS SHRINE AT SANTIAGO DE COMPOSTELLA IN GALICIA. THE FLAMED SCALLOPS ARE COVERED IN TOMATO SAUCE AND ARE SERVED HOT IN THE CURVED SHELL, WITH CRISP BREADCRUMBS ON TOP.

SERVES FOUR

INGREDIENTS
   30ml/2 tbsp olive oil
   1 onion, finely chopped
   2 garlic cloves, finely chopped
   200g/7oz can tomatoes
   pinch of cayenne pepper
   45ml/3 tbsp finely chopped
      fresh parsley
   50ml/2fl oz/¼ cup orange juice
   50g/2oz/4 tbsp butter
   450g/1lb large shelled scallops,
      or 8–12 large ones on the shell,
      detached and cleaned
   30ml/2 tbsp anis spirit, such as
      Ricard or Pernod
   90ml/6 tbsp stale breadcrumbs
   salt and ground black pepper

1 Heat the oil in a pan and fry the onion and garlic over a gentle heat. Add the tomatoes and cook for 10–15 minutes, stirring occasionally. Season with a little salt and cayenne pepper.

2 Transfer the tomato mixture to a small food processor or blender, add 30ml/ 2 tbsp of the parsley and the orange juice and blend to form a smooth purée.

3 Preheat the grill (broiler) with the shelf at its highest. Arrange four curved scallop shells, or flameproof ramekin dishes, on a baking tray.

4 Heat 25g/1oz/2 tbsp of the butter in a small frying pan and fry the scallops gently, for about 2 minutes, or until sealed but not totally cooked through.

5 Pour the anis spirit into a ladle and set light to it. Pour over the scallops and shake the pan gently until the flames die down. Divide the scallops among the prepared shells (or dishes) and salt them lightly. Add the pan juices to the tomato sauce.

6 Pour the tomato sauce over the scallops. Mix together the breadcrumbs and the remaining parsley, season very lightly and sprinkle over the top.

7 Melt the remaining butter in a small pan and drizzle over the breadcrumbs. Grill (broil) the scallops for about 1 minute to colour the tops and heat through. Serve immediately.

COOK'S TIP
If you can lay your hands on the curved shells of scallops, wash and keep them after use. Fresh scallops are usually sold on the flat shell so the second shell, which can be used as a little dish, is now quite a rarity.

FLASH-FRIED SQUID WITH PAPRIKA AND GARLIC

SQUID ARE PART OF EVERY TAPAS BAR SELECTION, AND ARE USUALLY DEEP-FRIED. HERE IS A MODERN RECIPE, WHICH IS UNUSUAL IN THAT IT USES FRESH CHILLIES. SERVE THE DISH WITH A FINO OR MANZANILLA SHERRY AS A TAPAS DISH. ALTERNATIVELY, SERVE THE CALAMARES ON A BED OF SALAD LEAVES, ACCOMPANIED BY BREAD, FOR A SUBSTANTIAL FIRST COURSE TO SERVE FOUR.

SERVES SIX TO EIGHT

INGREDIENTS

- 500g/1¼lb very small squid, cleaned
- 90ml/6 tbsp olive oil, plus extra
- 1 fresh red chilli, seeded and finely chopped
- 10ml/2 tsp Spanish mild smoked paprika
- 30ml/2 tbsp plain (all-purpose) flour
- 2 garlic cloves, finely chopped
- 15ml/1 tbsp sherry vinegar
- 5ml/1 tsp grated lemon rind
- 30–45ml/2–3 tbsp finely chopped fresh parsley
- salt and ground black pepper

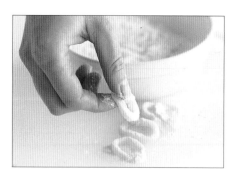

3 Toss the squid in the flour and divide it into two batches. Heat the remaining oil in a wok or deep frying pan over a high heat until very hot. Add the first batch of squid and quickly stir-fry for 1–2 minutes, or until it becomes opaque and the tentacles curl.

4 Add half the garlic. Stir, then turn out into a bowl. Repeat with the second batch, adding more oil if needed.

5 Sprinkle with the sherry vinegar, lemon rind, remaining chilli and parsley. Season and serve hot or cool.

1 Using a sharp knife, cut the squid body sacs into rings and cut the tentacles into bitesize pieces.

2 Place the squid in a bowl and pour over 30ml/2 tbsp of the olive oil, half the chilli and the paprika. Season with a little salt and some pepper, cover with clear film (plastic wrap), place in the refrigerator and leave to marinate for 2–4 hours.

COOK'S TIPS

• Make sure the oil in the pan is very hot before adding the squid. The squid should cook for only 1–2 minutes; any longer and it will begin to toughen.

• Smoked paprika, chiefly from the Valle de Jerte, has a wonderful, subtle flavour. If you cannot find it, you can use mild paprika instead.

CALAMARES RELLENOS

*SQUID ARE OFTEN JUST STUFFED WITH THEIR OWN TENTACLES BUT, IN THIS RECIPE, HAM AND RAISINS,
WHICH CONTRAST WONDERFULLY WITH THE SUBTLE FLAVOUR OF THE SQUID, ARE ALSO INCLUDED.
THE STUFFED SQUID ARE COOKED IN A RICHLY FLAVOURED TOMATO SAUCE AND MAKE A PERFECT
APPETIZER. TO SERVE AS A MAIN COURSE, SIMPLY ACCOMPANY WITH PLAIN BOILED RICE.*

SERVES FOUR

INGREDIENTS

2 squid, about 275g/10oz each
60ml/4 tbsp olive oil
1 small onion, finely chopped
2 garlic cloves, finely chopped
50g/2oz Serrano ham or gammon
  steak, diced small
75g/3oz/scant ½ cup long grain rice
30ml/2 tbsp raisins, chopped
30ml/2 tbsp finely chopped
  fresh parsley
½ small (US medium) egg, beaten
plain (all-purpose) flour, for dusting
250ml/8fl oz/1 cup white wine
1 bay leaf
30ml/2 tbsp chopped fresh parsley
salt, paprika and black pepper
For the tomato sauce
30ml/2 tbsp olive oil
1 onion, finely chopped
2 garlic cloves, finely chopped
200g/7oz can tomatoes
salt and cayenne pepper

1 Make the tomato sauce. Heat the oil in a flameproof casserole large enough to hold the squid. Cook the onion and garlic over a gentle heat. Add the tomatoes and cook for 10–15 minutes. Season with salt and cayenne pepper.

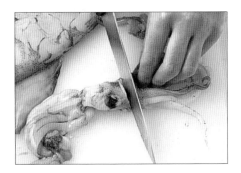

2 To prepare the squid, use the tentacles to pull out the body. Cut off the tentacles, discarding the eyes and everything below. Flex the bodies to pop out the spinal structure. Chop the fin flaps and rinse the bodies well.

3 Heat half the oil in a pan and gently fry the onion and garlic together. Add the ham and squid tentacles and stir-fry. Off the heat stir in the rice, chopped raisins and parsley. Season well and add the egg to bind the ingredients.

4 Spoon the mixture into the squid bodies, then stitch each of them shut using a small poultry skewer. Blot the bodies with kitchen paper, then flour them very lightly. Heat the remaining oil in a frying pan and fry the squid, turning until coloured on all sides.

5 Move the squid with two spoons and arrange them in the tomato sauce. Add the wine and bay leaf. Cover the casserole tightly and simmer for about 30 minutes, turning the squid over halfway through cooking if the sauce does not cover them completely. Serve sliced into rings, surrounded by the sauce and garnished with parsley.

MEAT AND POULTRY DISHES

There is a huge choice of good-quality meat available in Spain, and it is used to prepare all sorts of dishes. Pork is especially popular for sausages and tapas dishes and is used to make morcilla, lomo, jamón, chorizo, fuet, salchichón *and* salchichas.

RIÑONES AL JEREZ

KIDNEYS COOKED IN SHERRY ARE EXTREMELY POPULAR IN TAPAS BARS, AND MAKE AN EXCELLENT FAMILY SUPPER. AS A FIRST COURSE, PARTNER THE DISH WITH FRIED TOAST TRIANGLES OR CRUSTY BREAD. A FINO MONTILLA WINE, LESS WELL KNOWN THAN SHERRY BUT WITH THE SAME DRY QUALITIES, COULD REPLACE THE SHERRY. C.B. MONTILLA IS OFTEN THE CHOICE IN ANDALUSIA FOR THIS DISH.

SERVES FOUR

INGREDIENTS
  12 plump lamb's kidneys
  60ml/4 tbsp olive oil
  115g/4oz smoked bacon lardons,
    or diced pancetta
  1 large onion, chopped
  2 garlic cloves, finely chopped
  30ml/2 tbsp plain (all-purpose) flour
  150ml/¼ pint/⅔ cup fino sherry
    or C.B. Montilla wine
  15ml/1 tbsp tomato purée (paste)
  30ml/2 tbsp chopped fresh parsley
  salt and ground black pepper
  new potatoes, boiled and buttered,
    to serve (optional)

1 Halve and skin the kidneys, then remove the cores. Cut the kidneys into cubes. Heat half the oil in a large frying pan and fry the bacon or pancetta until the fat starts to run. Add the onion and garlic and fry until softened. Remove to a plate.

2 Add the remaining oil to the pan and divide the kidneys into four batches. Put in one handful, and stir-fry over a high heat until sealed. (They should not give off any juice.) Remove to a plate and repeat with a second handful and remove to the plate. Continue until they are all cooked.

3 Return the onion and bacon mixture to the pan. Sprinkle with flour and cook, stirring gently. Add the sherry or Montilla wine and stir until thickened. Add the tomato purée and parsley. Return the kidneys to the pan, and heat through. Season well and serve hot with buttered new potatoes, if you like.

PINCHITOS MORUÑOS

The Moors introduced both skewers and marinated meat to Spain. These little yellow kebabs are a favourite in Andalusia, where many butchers sell the meat ready marinated. The Arab versions used lamb, but pork is used now, because the spicing fits so perfectly.

SERVES FOUR

INGREDIENTS
  2.5ml/½ tsp cumin seeds
  2.5ml/½ tsp coriander seeds
  2 garlic cloves, finely chopped
  5ml/1 tsp paprika
  2.5ml/½ tsp dried oregano
  15ml/1 tbsp lemon juice
  45ml/3 tbsp olive oil
  500g/1¼lb lean cubed pork
  salt and ground black pepper

1 Starting a couple of hours in advance, grind the cumin and coriander seeds in a mortar and work in the garlic with a pinch of salt. Add the paprika and oregano and mix in the lemon juice. Stir in the oil.

2 Cut the pork into small cubes, then skewer them, three or four at a time, on to cocktail sticks (toothpicks). Put the skewered meat in a shallow dish, and pour over the marinade. Spoon the marinade back over the meat to ensure it is well coated. Leave to marinate in a cool place for 2 hours.

3 Preheat the grill (broiler) to high, and line the grill pan with foil. Spread the kebabs out in a row and place under the grill, close to the heat. Cook for about 3 minutes on each side, spooning the juices over when you turn them, until cooked through. Sprinkle with salt and pepper, and serve at once.

FRIED BLACK PUDDING

SPANISH MORCILLA — BLACK PUDDING — IS THE FIRST SAUSAGE TO BE MADE FROM THE FRESHLY KILLED PIG AND IS VERY POPULAR THROUGHOUT SPAIN. IT IS FLAVOURED WITH SPICES AND HERBS, USUALLY INCLUDING GARLIC AND OREGANO, AND HAS A WONDERFULLY RICH, SPICY TASTE.

SERVES FOUR

INGREDIENTS
15ml/1 tbsp olive oil
1 onion, thinly sliced
2 garlic cloves, thinly sliced
5ml/1 tsp dried oregano
5ml/1 tsp paprika
225g/8oz black pudding (blood
    sausage), cut into 12 thick slices
1 thin French stick, sliced into 12
30ml/2 tbsp fino sherry
sugar, to taste
salt and ground black pepper
chopped fresh oregano, to garnish

COOK'S TIP
If you can find real *morcilla*, serve it neat: simply fry the slices in olive oil and use to top little rounds of bread. If you cannot find black pudding, you can use red chorizo instead.

1 Heat the olive oil in a large frying pan and fry the sliced onion, garlic, oregano and paprika for 7–8 minutes until the onion is softened and has turned golden brown.

2 Add the slices of black pudding, then increase the heat and cook them for 3 minutes, without stirring. Turn them over carefully with a spatula and cook for a further 3 minutes until crisp.

3 Arrange the rounds of bread on a large serving plate and top each with a slice of black pudding. Stir the sherry into the onions and add a little sugar to taste. Heat, swirling the mixture around the pan until bubbling, then season with salt and black pepper.

4 Spoon a little of the onion mixture on top of each slice of black pudding. Scatter the oregano over and serve.

BARBECUED MINI RIBS

THESE TASTY RIBS ARE KNOWN AS COSTILLAS IN SPAIN. THEY ARE DELICIOUS COOKED ON A BARBECUE AND ALMOST AS GOOD WHEN COOKED UNDER A HOT GRILL. IF YOU PREFER A SWEETER FLAVOUR, USE FRESHLY SQUEEZED ORANGE JUICE INSTEAD OF THE SWEET SHERRY.

SERVES SIX TO EIGHT

INGREDIENTS

1 sheet of pork ribs, about 675g/1½lb
90ml/6 tbsp sweet oloroso sherry
15ml/1 tbsp tomato purée (paste)
5ml/1 tsp soy sauce
2.5ml/½ tsp Tabasco sauce
15ml/1 tbsp light muscovado (brown) sugar
30ml/2 tbsp seasoned plain (all-purpose) flour
coarse sea salt

COOK'S TIP
Oloroso sherry has a full body and sweet flavour sometimes reminiscent of port.

1 Separate the ribs, then, using a meat cleaver or heavy knife, cut each rib in half widthways to make about 30 pieces.

2 Mix the sherry, tomato purée, soy sauce, Tabasco and sugar in a bowl. Stir in 2.5ml/½ tsp salt.

3 Put the seasoned flour in a strong plastic bag, then add the ribs and toss to coat. Dip each rib in the sauce. Cook on a hot barbecue or under a hot grill (broiler) for 30–40 minutes, turning occasionally until cooked and a little charred. Sprinkle with salt and serve.

CHORIZO WITH CHESTNUTS

CHESTNUTS ARE NATIVE TO GALICIA AND ARE A POPULAR ADDITION TO A VARIETY OF DISHES. CHORIZOS Y CASTANAS MAKES A GOOD SIDE DISH FOR ROAST TURKEY AND A POPULAR SUPPER DISH SERVED ON ITS OWN. ADD A LITTLE CHILLI IF YOU LIKE THINGS HOT AND SPICY.

SERVES THREE TO SIX

INGREDIENTS
    15ml/1 tbsp olive oil
    4 red chorizo sausages, sliced
    200g/7oz/1¼ cups peeled
        cooked chestnuts
    15ml/1 tbsp paprika
    salt and ground black pepper
    crusty bread, to serve

COOK'S TIP
In Spain, chorizo for frying is sold as red links. Both mild and spicy types are available. Similar kinds of red sausage are made in Italy and Mexico.

1 Heat the oil in a wide frying pan and put in the chorizo slices in a single layer. Cook the chorizo for 3–4 minutes, turning frequently, until it starts to give off its oil.

2 Tip in the peeled chestnuts and toss until warm and covered with the chorizo oil. Add the paprika and season with salt and ground black pepper. Serve hot with crusty bread.

ALBÓNDIGAS CON SALSA DE TOMATE

SPANISH MEN LIKE TO FIND TRADITIONAL DISHES IN THEIR FAVOURITE TAPAS BAR. THESE TASTY MEATBALLS IN TOMATO SAUCE ARE USUALLY SERVED IN LITTLE BROWN, INDIVIDUAL CASSEROLE DISHES, ACCOMPANIED BY CRUSTY BREAD. THEY MAKE A GOOD SUPPER, TOO, WITH A GREEN SALAD OR PASTA.

SERVES FOUR

INGREDIENTS
    225g/8oz minced (ground) beef
    4 spring onions (scallions),
        thinly sliced
    2 garlic cloves, finely chopped
    30ml/2 tbsp grated fresh
        Parmesan cheese
    10ml/2 tsp fresh thyme leaves
    15ml/1 tbsp olive oil
    3 tomatoes, chopped
    30ml/2 tbsp red or dry white wine
    10ml/2 tsp chopped fresh rosemary
    pinch of sugar
    salt and ground black pepper
    fresh thyme, to garnish

1 Put the minced beef in a bowl. Add the spring onions, garlic, Parmesan and thyme and plenty of salt and pepper.

2 Stir well to combine, then shape the mixture into 12 small firm balls.

3 Heat the olive oil in a large, heavy frying pan and cook the meatballs for about 5 minutes, turning frequently, until evenly browned all over.

4 Add the chopped tomatoes, wine, rosemary and sugar to the pan, with salt and ground black pepper to taste.

5 Cover the pan and cook gently for about 15 minutes until the tomatoes are pulpy and the meatballs are cooked through. Check the sauce for seasoning and serve the meatballs hot, garnished with the thyme.

VARIATION
Albóndigas are equally good made of half beef and half pork, or a mixture of meats, including ham. In the sausage-making areas, particularly Extremadura, they may be made completely of pork. Meatballs, called *la prueba* ("the try-out"), are made to test the seasoning.

VARIATION
To make *biftek andaluz* (the nearest thing Spain has to a beefburger), shape the meat mixture into four wide patties and fry. Serve the patties on a slice of grilled (broiled) beefsteak tomato, or surrounded by tomato sauce. Top with a fried egg for decoration, if you like.

SPICY SAUSAGE AND CHEESE TORTILLA

THIS SUBSTANTIAL TORTILLA IS DELICIOUS HOT OR COLD. CUT IT INTO CHUNKY WEDGES AND SERVE FOR SUPPER OR A LIGHT LUNCH WITH A FRESH TOMATO AND BASIL SALAD. THE ADDITION OF SPICY CHORIZO AND TANGY CHEESE GIVES IT A WONDERFUL, RICH FLAVOUR.

2 Add a further 30ml/2 tbsp oil to the pan and fry the potatoes and onions for 2–3 minutes, turning frequently (the pan will be very full). Cover tightly and cook over a gentle heat for about 30 minutes, turning occasionally, until softened and slightly golden.

3 In a large mixing bowl, beat together the eggs, parsley, cheese, sausage and plenty of seasoning. Gently stir in the potatoes and onions until coated, taking care not to break up the potato too much.

4 Wipe out the pan with kitchen paper and heat the remaining 30ml/2 tbsp oil. Add the potato mixture and cook, over a very low heat, until the egg begins to set. Use a metal spatula to prevent the tortilla from sticking and allow the uncooked egg to run underneath.

5 Preheat the grill (broiler) to high. When the base of the tortilla has set, which should take about 5 minutes, protect the pan handle with foil and place the tortilla under the grill until it is set and golden. Cut into wedges and serve garnished with parsley.

SERVES FOUR TO SIX

INGREDIENTS
- 75ml/5 tbsp olive oil
- 175g/6oz frying chorizo or spicy sausage, thinly sliced
- 675g/1½lb waxy potatoes, thinly sliced
- 2 Spanish onions, halved and thinly sliced
- 4 large (US extra large) eggs
- 30ml/2 tbsp chopped fresh parsley, plus extra to garnish
- 115g/4oz/1 cup grated Cheddar or other hard cheese
- salt and ground black pepper

1 Heat 15ml/1 tbsp of the oil in a 20cm/8in non-stick frying pan and fry the sausage until golden brown and cooked through. Lift out with a slotted spoon and drain on kitchen paper.

CHORIZO WITH GARLIC POTATOES

A CLASSIC TAPAS RECIPE, THIS SIMPLE BUT RICH GARLICKY DISH CAN BE SERVED IN SMALL QUANTITIES AS A SNACK OR, AS HERE, IN SLIGHTLY LARGER PROPORTIONS FOR AN APPETIZER OR TO ACCOMPANY A MAIN COURSE DISH.

SERVES FOUR

INGREDIENTS

    450g/1lb potatoes
    3 eggs, hard-boiled and quartered
    175g/6oz chorizo sausage, sliced
    150ml/¼ pint/⅔ cup mayonnaise
    150ml/¼ pint/⅔ cup sour cream
    2 garlic cloves, crushed
    salt and ground black pepper
    30ml/2 tbsp chopped fresh
        coriander (cilantro), to garnish

VARIATION
To give this dish a more piquant flavour, add about 15ml/1 tbsp finely chopped cornichons and 4 finely chopped anchovy fillets. If coriander isn't available, then use 15ml/1 tbsp fresh marjoram instead.

1 Cook the potatoes in a pan of boiling salted water for 20 minutes, or until tender. Drain and leave to cool.

2 Cut the potatoes into bite-size pieces. Place them in a large serving dish with the eggs and chorizo sausage, and season to taste with salt and pepper.

3 In a small bowl, stir the mayonnaise, sour cream and garlic together with seasoning to taste, then spoon this dressing over the potato mixture.

4 Toss the salad gently to coat the ingredients with dressing, then sprinkle with chopped coriander to garnish.

CHICKEN WITH LEMON AND GARLIC

POLLO CON LIMÓN Y AJILLO *IS ONE OF THE SIMPLEST AND MOST DELICIOUS WAYS TO SERVE CHICKEN. IT MAKES A GOOD TAPAS DISH, SERVED WITH COCKTAIL STICKS TO PICK UP THE LITTLE STRIPS OF RICHLY FLAVOURED CHICKEN, OR A SUPPER FOR TWO, WITH FRIED POTATOES.*

SERVES TWO TO FOUR

INGREDIENTS
2 skinless chicken breast fillets
30ml/2 tbsp olive oil
1 shallot, finely chopped
4 garlic cloves, finely chopped
5ml/1 tsp paprika
juice of 1 lemon
30ml/2 tbsp chopped fresh parsley
salt and ground black pepper
fresh flat leaf parsley, to garnish
lemon wedges, to serve

VARIATION
For a variation on this dish, try using strips of turkey breast or pork fillet. They need slightly longer cooking. The whites of spring onions (scallions) can replace shallots, and the chopped green tops replace the parsley.

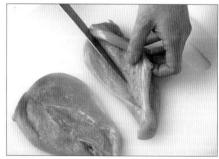

1 Remove the little fillet from the back of each breast. If the breast still looks fatter than a finger, bat it with a rolling pin to make it thinner. Slice all the chicken meat into strips.

2 Heat the oil in a large frying pan. Stir-fry the chicken strips with the shallot, garlic and paprika over a high heat for about 3 minutes until cooked through.

3 Add the lemon juice and parsley and season with salt and pepper to taste. Serve hot with lemon wedges, garnished with flat leaf parsley.

COOK'S TIP
Chicken breasts have a little fillet strip that easily becomes detached. Collect these, in a bag or container in the freezer, for this dish.

CHICKEN LIVERS <u>IN</u> SHERRY

HIGADILLAS CON JEREZ IS VERY POPULAR, MADE WITH TRADITIONAL SPANISH INGREDIENTS. IT MAKES A DELICIOUS LITTLE TAPAS DISH AND IS PARTICULARLY GOOD EATEN WITH BREAD OR ON TOAST. FOR A MORE ELEGANT PRESENTATION, SERVE PILED ON TOP OF LITTLE RICE TORTITAS.

SERVES FOUR

INGREDIENTS

   225g/8oz chicken livers, thawed
     if frozen, trimmed
   15ml/1 tbsp olive oil
   1 small onion, finely chopped
   2 small garlic cloves, finely chopped
   5ml/1 tsp fresh thyme leaves
   30ml/2 tbsp sweet oloroso sherry
   30ml/2 tbsp crème fraîche or double
     (heavy) cream
   2.5ml/½ tsp paprika
   salt and ground black pepper
   fresh thyme, to garnish

1 Trim any green spots and sinews from the chicken livers. Heat the oil in a frying pan and fry the onion, garlic, chicken livers and thyme for 3 minutes.

2 Stir the sherry into the livers, then add the cream and cook briefly. Season with salt, pepper and paprika, garnish with thyme and serve immediately.

CHICKEN CROQUETTES

CROQUETAS ARE VERY POPULAR TAPAS FARE AND THERE ARE MANY DIFFERENT VARIATIONS. THIS ONE IS BASED ON BECHAMEL SAUCE, WHICH IS PERFECT FOR TAKING ON DIFFERENT FLAVOURS SUCH AS HAM OR CHOPPED PEPPERS. THE CROQUETTES ARE BEST FRIED JUST BEFORE SERVING.

SERVES FOUR

INGREDIENTS
    25g/1oz/2 tbsp butter
    25g/1oz/¼ cup plain
      (all-purpose) flour
    150ml/¼ pint/⅔ cup milk
    15ml/1 tbsp olive oil, plus extra
      for deep-frying
    1 boneless chicken breast
      with skin, diced
    1 garlic clove, finely chopped
    1 small egg, beaten
    50g/2oz/1 cup stale white
      breadcrumbs
    salt and ground black pepper
    fresh flat leaf parsley, to garnish
    lemon wedges, to serve

1 Melt the butter in a pan. Add the flour and cook gently, stirring, for 1 minute. Gradually stir in the milk and cook until smooth and thick. Cover and set aside.

2 Heat the oil in a frying pan and fry the chicken and garlic for 5 minutes.

3 When the chicken is lightly browned and cooked through, tip the contents of the frying pan into a food processor and process until finely chopped. Tip the mixture into the sauce and stir to combine. Season with plenty of salt and pepper to taste, then set aside to cool completely.

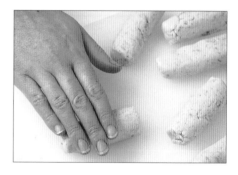

4 Once cooled and firm, shape the mixture into eight small sausage shapes. Dip each one in beaten egg, then roll in breadcrumbs to coat.

5 Heat the oil in a large pan, until a cube of bread dropped in the oil browns in 1 minute. Lower the croquettes into the oil and cook for 4 minutes until crisp and golden. Lift out using a slotted spoon and drain on kitchen paper. Serve with lemon wedges and garnish with fresh flat leaf parsley.

ORANGE CHICKEN SALAD

WITH THEIR TANGY FLAVOUR, ORANGE SEGMENTS ARE THE PERFECT PARTNER FOR TENDER CHICKEN IN THIS TASTY RICE SALAD. TO APPRECIATE ALL THE FLAVOURS FULLY, SERVE THE SALAD AT ROOM TEMPERATURE. IT MAKES THE PERFECT DISH FOR A HOT SUMMER DAY.

SERVES FOUR

INGREDIENTS

3 large seedless oranges
175g/6oz/scant 1 cup long grain rice
10ml/2 tsp strong Dijon mustard
2.5ml/½ tsp caster (superfine) sugar
175ml/6fl oz/¾ cup vinaigrette
450g/1lb cooked chicken, diced
45ml/3 tbsp chopped fresh chives
75g/3oz/¾ cup almonds or cashew
  nuts, toasted
salt and ground black pepper
mixed salad leaves, to serve

COOK'S TIP
To make a simple vinaigrette, whisk
45ml/3 tbsp wine vinegar with 90ml/
6 tbsp olive oil. Add 60ml/4 tbsp extra
virgin olive oil and season well.

1 Pare one of the oranges thinly, removing only the rind, not the white pith. Put the pieces of orange rind in a pan and add the rice. Pour in 475ml/ 16fl oz/2 cups water, add a pinch of salt and bring to the boil. Cover and cook over a very low heat for about 15 minutes, or until the rice is tender and all the water has been absorbed.

2 Meanwhile, peel the oranges, removing all the white pith. Working over a plate to catch the juices, separate them into segments. Tip in the orange juice from the plate and add to the vinaigrette with the mustard and sugar, whisking to combine. Check the seasoning.

3 When the rice is cooked, remove it from the heat and discard the pieces of orange rind. Spoon the rice into a bowl, let it cool slightly, then add half the dressing. Toss well, then set aside to cool completely.

4 Add the chicken, chives, toasted nuts and orange segments to the cooled rice. Pour over the remaining dressing and toss gently to combine. Serve on a bed of mixed salad leaves.

VEGETABLE SNACKS

*Vegetable dishes in Spain are inventive and are often eaten as a
tapas dish, a course on their own, or perhaps as a supper.
Simple ingredients are cleverly paired to show off their
qualities to perfection and are typical of Spain's attitude
to cooking, using fresh, local seasonal ingredients. They often
include meat as there is little purely vegetarian cooking.*

POTATO TORTILLA

THE CLASSIC TORTILLA STANDS ON EVERY TAPAS BAR IN SPAIN. THE SIZE OF A LARGE CAKE, IT IS DENSE AND VERY SATISFYING. IT CAN BE EATEN IN WEDGES WITH A FORK — A MEAL IN ITSELF WITH SALAD — OR CUT UP INTO CHUNKS AND SPEARED, TO BE ENJOYED AS A SNACK WITH DRINKS.

SERVES SIX

INGREDIENTS
    450g/1lb small waxy potatoes, peeled
    1 Spanish onion
    45ml/3 tbsp vegetable oil
    4 large (US extra large) eggs
    salt and ground black pepper
    fresh flat leaf parsley or tomato
     wedges, to garnish

1 Using a sharp knife, cut the potatoes into thin slices and slice the onion into thin rings. Heat 30ml/2 tbsp of the oil in a 20cm/8in heavy frying pan.

2 Add the potatoes and the onions to the pan and cook over a low heat for 20 minutes, or until the potato slices are just tender. Remove from the heat.

3 In a large bowl, beat together the eggs with a little salt and pepper. Stir in the cooked potatoes and onion.

4 Clean the frying pan with kitchen paper then heat the remaining oil and pour in the potato mixture. Cook very gently for 5–8 minutes until set underneath. During cooking, lift the edges of the tortilla with a spatula, and allow any uncooked egg to run underneath. Shake the pan from side to side, to prevent sticking.

5 Place a large heatproof plate upside-down over the pan, invert the tortilla on to the plate and then slide it back into the pan. Cook for 2–3 minutes more, until the underside of the tortilla is golden brown. Cut into wedges and serve, garnished with fresh flat leaf parsley or tomato wedges.

TORTILLA <u>WITH</u> BEANS

THE ADDITION OF CHOPPED HERBS AND A FEW SKINNED BEANS TO THE CLASSIC TORTILLA MAKES THIS A VERY SUMMERY DISH. ENJOY IT AS A LIGHT LUNCH, OR CUT IT INTO SMALL PIECES AND SERVE AS A TAPAS DISH. TORTILLA IS A MUST IN TAPAS SELECTIONS.

SERVES TWO

INGREDIENTS
- 45ml/3 tbsp olive oil
- 2 Spanish onions, thinly sliced
- 300g/11oz waxy potatoes, cut into dice
- 250g/9oz/1¾ cups shelled broad (fava) beans
- 5ml/1 tsp chopped fresh thyme or summer savory
- 6 large (US extra large) eggs
- 45ml/3 tbsp mixed chopped fresh chives and fresh flat leaf parsley
- salt and ground black pepper

1 Heat 30ml/2 tbsp of the oil in a 23cm/9in deep non-stick frying pan. Add the onions and potatoes and stir to coat. Cover and cook gently, stirring, for 20–25 minutes until the potatoes are cooked and the onions collapsed.

2 Meanwhile, cook the beans in a pan of boiling salted water for 5 minutes. Drain well and set aside to cool.

3 When the beans are cool enough to handle, peel off and discard the grey outer skins. Add the beans to the frying pan, together with the thyme or summer savory and season with salt and pepper to taste. Stir well to mix and cook for a further 2–3 minutes.

4 Beat the eggs with salt and pepper to taste and add the mixed herbs. Pour the egg mixture over the potatoes and onions and increase the heat slightly. Cook gently for about 5 minutes, or until the egg on the bottom sets and browns. During cooking, gently pull the tortilla away from the sides of the pan and tilt to allow the uncooked egg to run underneath.

5 Cover the frying pan with a large, upside-down plate and invert the tortilla on to it. Add the remaining oil to the pan and heat until hot. Slip the tortilla back into the pan, uncooked side down, and cook for 3–5 minutes until the underneath browns.

6 Slide the tortilla out on to a plate. Cut up into wedges or cubes and serve warm rather than piping hot.

POTATO AND RED PEPPER FRITTATA

FRITTATA IS LIKE A LARGE OMELETTE, THIS TASTY VERSION IS FILLED WITH POTATOES AND PLENTY OF HERBS. DO USE FRESH MINT IN PREFERENCE TO DRIED IF YOU CAN FIND IT.

SERVES THREE TO FOUR

INGREDIENTS
   450g/1lb small new or
      salad potatoes
   6 eggs
   30ml/2 tbsp chopped fresh mint
   30ml/2 tbsp olive oil
   1 onion, chopped
   2 garlic cloves, crushed
   2 red (bell) peppers, seeded and
      roughly chopped
   salt and ground black pepper
   mint sprigs, to garnish

1 Cook the potatoes in their skins in boiling salted water until just tender. Drain and leave to cool slightly, then cut into thick slices.

2 Whisk together the eggs, mint and seasoning in a bowl, then set aside. Heat the oil in a large frying pan.

3 Add the onion, garlic, peppers and potatoes to the pan and cook, stirring occasionally, for 5 minutes.

4 Pour the egg mixture over the vegetables in the frying pan and stir gently.

5 Push the mixture towards the centre of the pan as it cooks to allow the liquid egg to run on to the base. Meanwhile preheat the grill.

6 When the frittata is lightly set, place the pan under the hot grill for 2–3 minutes until the top is a light golden brown colour.

7 Serve hot or cold, cut into wedges piled high on a serving dish and garnished with sprigs of mint.

CHEESE TORTILLA WITH TOMATO SALSA

GOOD WARM OR COLD, THIS IS LIKE A SLICED POTATO QUICHE WITHOUT THE PASTRY BASE,
WELL SPIKED WITH CHILLI. THE SALSA CAN BE MADE WITHOUT THE CHILLI IF YOU PREFER.

SERVES FOUR

INGREDIENTS

45ml/3 tbsp sunflower or olive oil
1 small onion, thinly sliced
2–3 fresh green jalapeño chillies,
 seeded and sliced
200g/7oz cold cooked potato,
 thinly sliced
120g/4¼oz/generous 1 cup cheese,
 grated (use a firm but not hard
 cheese, such as Double Gloucester,
 Monterey Jack or Manchego)
6 eggs, beaten
salt and ground black pepper
fresh herbs, to garnish

For the salsa

500g/1¼lb fresh tomatoes, peeled,
 seeded and finely chopped
1 fresh mild green chilli, seeded
 and finely chopped
2 garlic cloves, crushed
45ml/3 tbsp chopped fresh
 coriander (cilantro)
juice of 1 lime
2.5ml/½ tsp salt

1 To make the fresh tomato salsa, put the chopped tomatoes in a large bowl and add the chopped chilli, garlic, coriander, lime juice and salt. Mix well and set aside.

2 Heat 15ml/1 tbsp of the oil in a large omelette pan and gently fry the onion and jalapeño chillies for 5 minutes, stirring until softened. Add the sliced potato and gently cook for 5 minutes until lightly browned, keeping the slices whole.

3 Using a slotted spoon, transfer the vegetables to a warm plate. Wipe the pan with kitchen paper, then add the remaining oil and heat until really hot. Return the vegetables to the pan. Scatter the cheese over the top. Season.

4 Pour in the beaten eggs, making sure that they seep under the vegetables. Cook the tortilla over a low heat, without stirring, until set. Serve hot or cold, cut into wedges, garnished with fresh herbs and with the salsa on the side.

RICE TORTITAS

LIKE MINIATURE TORTILLAS, THESE LITTLE RICE PANCAKES ARE GOOD SERVED HOT, EITHER PLAIN OR WITH TOMATO SAUCE FOR DIPPING. THEY MAKE AN EXCELLENT SCOOP FOR ANY SOFT VEGETABLE MIXTURE OR DIP — A VERY SPANISH WAY OF EATING.

SERVES FOUR

INGREDIENTS
   30ml/2 tbsp olive oil
   115g/4oz/1 cup cooked long grain
    white rice
   1 potato, grated
   4 spring onions (scallions),
    thinly sliced
   1 garlic clove, finely chopped
   15ml/1 tbsp chopped fresh parsley
   3 large (US extra large)
    eggs, beaten
   2.5ml/½ tsp paprika
   salt and ground black pepper

COOK'S TIP
These *tortitas* can be used as a base, for example for cooked chicken livers, instead of the usual sliced bread.

1 Heat half the olive oil in a large frying pan and stir-fry the rice, with the potato, spring onions and garlic, over a high heat for 3 minutes until golden.

2 Tip the rice and vegetable mixture into a bowl and stir in the parsley and eggs, with the paprika and plenty of salt and pepper. Mix well.

3 Heat the remaining oil in the frying pan and drop in large spoonfuls of the rice mixture, leaving room for spreading. Cook the *tortitas* for 1–2 minutes on each side.

4 Drain the *tortitas* on kitchen paper and keep hot while cooking the remaining mixture. Serve hot.

ARTICHOKE RICE CAKES <u>WITH</u> MANCHEGO

THESE UNUSUAL LITTLE CROQUETAS CONTAIN ARTICHOKE IN THE RICE MIXTURE, AND THEY BREAK OPEN TO REVEAL A MELTING CHEESE CENTRE. MANCHEGO IS MADE FROM SHEEP'S MILK AND HAS A TART FLAVOUR THAT GOES WONDERFULLY WITH THE DELICATE TASTE OF THE RICE CAKES.

SERVES SIX

INGREDIENTS

   1 large globe artichoke
   50g/2oz/¼ cup butter
   1 small onion, finely chopped
   1 garlic clove, finely chopped
   115g/4oz/⅔ cup paella rice
   450ml/¾ pint/scant 2 cups hot
    chicken stock
   50g/2oz/⅔ cup grated fresh
    Parmesan cheese
   150g/5oz Manchego cheese, very
    finely diced
   45–60ml/3–4 tbsp fine corn meal
   olive oil, for frying
   salt and ground black pepper
   fresh flat leaf parsley, to garnish

1 Remove the stalks, leaves and choke to leave just the heart of the artichoke; chop the heart finely.

2 Melt the butter in a pan and gently fry the chopped artichoke heart, onion and garlic for 5 minutes until softened. Stir in the rice and cook for about 1 minute.

3 Keeping the heat fairly high, gradually add the stock, stirring occasionally until all the liquid has been absorbed and the rice is cooked – this should take about 20 minutes. Season well, then stir in the Parmesan cheese. Transfer the mixture to a bowl. Leave to cool, then cover and chill for at least 2 hours.

4 Spoon about 15ml/1 tbsp of the mixture into the palm of one hand, flatten slightly, and place a few pieces of diced cheese in the centre. Shape the rice around the cheese to make a small ball. Flatten slightly, then roll in the corn meal, shaking off any excess. Repeat with the remaining mixture to make about 12 cakes.

5 Shallow fry the rice cakes in hot olive oil for 4–5 minutes until they are crisp and golden brown. Drain on kitchen paper and serve hot, garnished with flat leaf parsley.

COOK'S TIP
Manchego is a hard cheese very similar to Italian Parmesan.

BAKED MEDITERRANEAN VEGETABLES

TOMATOES AND PEPPERS WERE IMPORTED INTO SPAIN HUNDREDS OF YEARS AGO AND ARE NOW GROWN EVERYWHERE. CRISP AND GOLDEN CRUNCHY BATTER SURROUNDS THESE FRESH VEGETABLES, TURNING THEM INTO A SUBSTANTIAL APPETIZER. USE OTHER VEGETABLES INSTEAD IF YOU PREFER.

SERVES SIX

INGREDIENTS

1 small aubergine (eggplant),
   trimmed, halved and
   thickly sliced
1 medium (US large) egg
115g/4oz/1 cup plain
   (all-purpose) flour
300ml/½ pint/1¼ cups milk
30ml/2 tbsp fresh thyme leaves,
   or 10ml/2 tsp dried
1 red onion
2 large courgettes (zucchini)
1 red (bell) pepper
1 yellow (bell) pepper
60–75ml/4–5 tbsp sunflower oil
salt and ground black pepper
30ml/2 tbsp freshly grated
   Parmesan cheese and fresh herbs,
   to garnish

1 Place the aubergine in a colander or sieve, sprinkle generously with salt and leave for 10 minutes. Drain and pat dry on kitchen paper.

2 Meanwhile, to make the batter, beat the egg, then beat in the flour and milk to make a smooth paste. Blend in the rest of the milk, add the thyme leaves and seasoning and blend until smooth.

3 Leave the batter in a cool place until required. Quarter the onion, slice the courgettes and quarter the peppers.

4 Put the oil in a large roasting pan and heat through in the oven at 220°C/425°F/Gas 7. Add all the vegetables, turn in the fat to coat them well and return to the oven for 20 minutes, until they start to cook.

5 Give the batter another whisk then pour over the vegetables and return to the oven for 30 minutes. The batter will be well puffed up and golden. Reduce the heat to 190°C/375°F/Gas 5 for another 10–15 minutes, until crisp around the edges. Sprinkle with Parmesan cheese and herbs and serve.

COOK'S TIP
It is essential to get the fat in the dish really hot before adding the batter, or it will not rise well. Use a dish that is not too deep.

PIPERADA SANDWICH

THE BASQUE OMELETTE, PIPERADA, IS VERY DIFFERENT FROM THE CAKE-LIKE TORTILLA. IT OOZES BUTTER AND TOMATO JUICE, AND DOES NOT HOLD ITS SHAPE AT ALL. THAT IS WHY IT MAKES SUCH A SATISFYING FILLING FOR A BOCADILLA — THE SPANISH SPLIT-ROLL SANDWICH.

SERVES SIX

INGREDIENTS

120–150ml/8–10 tbsp olive oil
2 small onions, coarsely chopped
4 red, orange or yellow (bell)
  peppers, seeded and chopped
2 large garlic cloves, finely chopped
pinch of chilli or hot cayenne pepper
675g/1½lb ripe tomatoes, peeled,
  seeded and chopped
15ml/1 tbsp chopped fresh oregano
  or 5ml/1 tsp dried
1 long French loaf
25g/1oz/2 tbsp butter
6 large (US extra large)
  eggs, beaten
salt and ground black pepper
basil leaves, to garnish (optional)

1 Heat 60ml/4 tbsp of the oil in a large heavy frying pan. Add the onions and cook over a gentle heat, stirring occasionally, for about 5 minutes until they are softened but not coloured.

2 Add the peppers, garlic and chilli powder or cayenne pepper to the pan. Cook for a further 5 minutes, stirring, then add the tomatoes, seasoning and fresh or dried oregano. Cook over a moderate heat for 15–20 minutes until the peppers are soft and most of the liquid has evaporated.

VARIATION
If you prefer, serve the piperada as an open sandwich on toasted bread, rather than in a split French stick.

3 Preheat the oven to 200°C/400°F/ Gas 6. Cut the bread in half lengthways, trim off the ends, then cut into six equal pieces and brush with the remaining olive oil. Place the bread on baking trays and bake for 8–10 minutes until crisp and just turning golden.

4 Heat the butter in a pan until it bubbles, add the eggs and cook, stirring, until softly scrambled. Turn off the heat and stir in the pepper mixture. Divide evenly among the pieces of bread and sprinkle with the basil leaves, if using. Serve hot or warm.

SCRAMBLED EGGS <u>WITH</u> SPRING ASPARAGUS

REVUELTO DE ESPÁRRAGOS IS ONE OF THOSE DELICIOUS EGG DISHES THAT SHOW OFF NEW GREEN SPRING VEGETABLES TO PERFECTION. DELIGHTFULLY TENDER FRESH ASPARAGUS AND SWEET PEAS MAKE PERFECT PARTNERS TO LIGHTLY COOKED EGGS.

SERVES FOUR

INGREDIENTS
    1 bunch thin asparagus
    30–45ml/2–3 tbsp tiny raw
      mangetouts (snow peas)
    8 large (US extra large) eggs
    30ml/2 tbsp milk
    50g/2oz/¼ cup butter
    salt and ground black pepper
    sweet paprika, for dusting

VARIATION
Replace the asparagus with the mangetouts. String 150g/5oz mangetouts, then slice them diagonally into two or three pieces. Cook for 2 minutes.

1 Prepare the asparagus. Using a large sharp knife, cut off and discard any hard stems. Cut the stems into short lengths, keeping the tips separate. Shell some of the fatter mangetout pods, to extract the tiny peas.

2 Tip the stems into a pan of boiling water and simmer for 4 minutes. Add the asparagus tips, and cook for another 6 minutes. If including some pea pod strips, cook them for 2 minutes. Break the eggs into a bowl and beat together with the milk, salt and black pepper.

3 Melt the butter in a large frying pan and pour in the eggs, scrambling them by pulling the cooked outsides to the middle with a wooden spoon. When the eggs are almost cooked, drain the asparagus and pea pod strips, if using, and stir into the eggs. Sprinkle the peas over the top, and dust lightly with paprika. Serve immediately.

SCRAMBLED EGGS WITH SPRING ONIONS

THE SPANISH ARE PARTICULAR ABOUT EGGS, DISTINGUISHING BETWEEN A REVUELTO, WHICH USES SOFTLY-SET SCRAMBLED EGGS, AND THE MORE SOLID TORTILLA THAT IS COOKED UNTIL SET. THIS IS AN ECONOMICAL WAY OF USING A FEW SHELLFISH.

SERVES FOUR

INGREDIENTS
    1 bunch spring onions (scallions)
    25g/1oz/2 tbsp butter
    30ml/2 tbsp oil
    150g/5oz shelled prawns (shrimp)
    8 large (US extra large) eggs
    30ml/2 tbsp milk
    45ml/3 tbsp chopped fresh parsley
    salt and ground black pepper
    crusty bread, to serve

VARIATION
The green shoots from garlic bulbs are another very popular spring ingredient for this type of dish and can be used in place of the spring onions. Called *ajetes* in Spain, they lend a delicate flavour to eggs.

1 Chop the white of the spring onions and reserve, keeping it separate from 30ml/2 tbsp of the green tops.

2 Heat the butter and oil in a large frying pan. Add the spring onion white and cook briefly. Add the prawns and heat through. (If the prawns are raw, cook them for 2 minutes.)

3 Beat the eggs with the milk and then season. Turn the heat to medium-high and pour the egg mixture over the prawns. Cook for about 2 minutes, stirring with a wooden spoon.

4 Sprinkle with parsley and spring onion greens. Divide among four plates and serve immediately with crusty bread.

CHARRED ARTICHOKES WITH LEMON OIL DIP

YOUNG ARTICHOKES, ALCACHOFAS, ARE COOKED OVER THE FIRST BARBECUES OF THE SUMMER.
HOWEVER, THEY ARE ALSO VERY GOOD ROASTED IN THE OVEN. A ROAST HEAD OF GARLIC COMBINED
WITH OLIVE OIL MAKES A CLASSIC, MILD SAUCE — CON MOJETE — FOR VEGETABLES.

SERVES TWO TO FOUR

INGREDIENTS
   15ml/1 tbsp lemon juice or white
     wine vinegar
   2 globe artichokes
   45ml/3 tbsp olive oil
   sea salt
   sprigs of fresh flat leaf parsley,
     to garnish
For the lemon oil dip
   12 garlic cloves, unpeeled
   1 lemon
   45ml/3 tbsp extra virgin olive oil

COOK'S TIP
Artichokes are usually boiled, but if you
can get young, tender artichokes, they
are delicious roasted over a barbecue.

1 Preheat the oven to 200ºC/400ºF/
Gas 6. Stir the lemon juice or vinegar
into a bowl of cold water.

2 Cut each artichoke lengthways into
wedges. Pull the hairy choke out from
the centre of each wedge and drop the
wedges into the acidulated water.

3 Drain the artichokes and place in a
roasting pan with the garlic cloves. Toss
in the oil. Sprinkle with salt and roast
for 40 minutes, stirring once or twice,
until the artichokes are tender.

4 Meanwhile, make the dip. Pare away
two strips of rind from the lemon and
scrape away any pith. Place the rind in
a pan with water to cover. Simmer for
5 minutes, then drain, refresh in cold
water and chop roughly.

5 Arrange the artichokes on a plate and
set aside to cool for 5 minutes. Flatten
the garlic cloves so that the flesh pops
out of the skins. Transfer the garlic
flesh to a bowl, mash to a purée then
add the lemon rind. Squeeze the juice
from the lemon, then, using a fork,
whisk in the olive oil and lemon juice.

6 Serve the artichokes warm. Garnish
them with parsley and accompany them
with the lemon dip.

SPINACH WITH RAISINS AND PINE NUTS

RAISINS AND PINE NUTS ARE FREQUENT PARTNERS IN SPANISH RECIPES, AS THE PINE NUTS ARE ASTRINGENT YET RICH, THE RAISINS SWEET. HERE, TOSSED WITH WILTED SPINACH AND CROÛTONS, THEY MAKE A DELICIOUS SNACK OR MAIN MEAL ACCOMPANIMENT.

SERVES FOUR

INGREDIENTS
  50g/2oz/⅓ cup raisins, preferably
    Malaga raisins
  1 thick slice crusty white bread
  45ml/3 tbsp olive oil
  25g/1oz/¼ cup pine nuts
  500g/1¼lb young spinach,
    stalks removed
  2 garlic cloves, finely chopped
  salt and ground black pepper

VARIATION
Swiss chard, also known as spinach beet and leaf beet, may be used instead of the spinach. It has a very similar flavour to spinach, but the leaves require slightly longer cooking.

1 Put the raisins in a small bowl and pour over enough boiling water to cover. Leave the raisins to soak for about 10 minutes, then drain well.

2 Cut off the crusts and cut the bread into cubes. Heat 30ml/2 tbsp of the oil in a frying pan and fry the cubes of bread until golden. Drain.

3 Heat the remaining oil in the pan. Gently fry the pine nuts until just colouring. Add the spinach and garlic and cook quickly, turning the spinach until it has just wilted.

4 Add the raisins and season lightly. Transfer to a warmed dish. Scatter with the croûtons and serve immediately.

MARINATED MUSHROOMS

CHAMPIÑONES EN ESCABECHE *IS A GOOD WAY TO SERVE MUSHROOMS IN SUMMER, AND MAKES A REFRESHING ALTERNATIVE TO THE EVER-POPULAR MUSHROOMS FRIED IN GARLIC. SERVE WITH PLENTY OF CRUSTY BREAD TO MOP UP THE DELICIOUS JUICES.*

SERVES FOUR

INGREDIENTS
  30ml/2 tbsp olive oil
  1 small onion, very finely chopped
  1 garlic clove, finely chopped
  15ml/1 tbsp tomato purée (paste)
  50ml/2fl oz/¼ cup amontillado sherry
  50ml/2fl oz/¼ cup water
  2 cloves
  225g/8oz/3 cups button (white)
    mushrooms, trimmed
  salt and ground black pepper
  chopped fresh parsley, to garnish

VARIATION
In Spain, wild mushrooms, known as *setas*, are served in this way.

1 Heat the oil in a pan. Add the onion and garlic and cook until soft. Stir in the tomato purée, sherry, water and the cloves and season with salt and black pepper. Bring to the boil, cover and simmer gently for 45 minutes, adding more water if it becomes too dry.

2 Add the mushrooms to the pan, then cover and allow to simmer for about 5 minutes. Remove from the heat and allow to cool, still covered. Chill in the refrigerator overnight. Serve the mushrooms cold, sprinkled with the chopped fresh parsley.

ENSALADILLA

KNOWN AS RUSSIAN SALAD ELSEWHERE, THIS "SALAD OF LITTLE THINGS" BECAME EXTREMELY POPULAR DURING THE SPANISH CIVIL WAR IN THE 1930s, WHEN MORE EXPENSIVE INGREDIENTS WERE SCARCE. IT MAY EVEN HAVE BEEN INVENTED IN SPAIN — DESPITE ITS NAME.

SERVES FOUR

INGREDIENTS

8 new potatoes, scrubbed
  and quartered
1 large carrot, diced
115g/4oz fine green beans,
  cut into 2cm/¾in lengths
75g/3oz/¾ cup peas
½ Spanish onion, chopped
4 cornichons or small
  gherkins, sliced
1 small red (bell) pepper, seeded
  and diced
50g/2oz/½ cup pitted black olives
15ml/1 tbsp drained pickled capers
15ml/1 tbsp freshly squeezed
  lemon juice
30ml/2 tbsp chopped fresh fennel
  or parsley
salt and ground black pepper
For the *allioli*
2 garlic cloves, finely chopped
2.5ml/½ tsp salt
150ml/¼ pint/⅔ cup mayonnaise

VARIATION
This salad is delicious using any combination of chopped, cooked vegetables. Use whatever is available.

1 Make the *allioli*. Crush the garlic with the salt in a mortar and whisk or stir into the mayonnaise.

2 Cook the potatoes and diced carrot in a pan of boiling lightly salted water for 5–8 minutes until almost tender. Add the beans and peas to the pan and cook for 2 minutes, or until all the vegetables are tender. Drain well.

3 Tip the vegetables into a large bowl. Add the onion, cornichons or gherkins, red pepper, olives and capers. Stir in the *allioli* and season to taste with pepper and lemon juice.

4 Toss the vegetables and allioli together until well combined, check the seasoning and chill well. Serve garnished with fennel or parsley.

BRAISED CABBAGE WITH CHORIZO

CABBAGES — BERZAS — MARK THE LANDSCAPE IN GALICIA, WHERE THE HUGE VEGETABLES GROW MORE THAN HIP HIGH. THEY ARE POPULARLY COOKED IN STEWS IN THE MANY MOUNTAIN REGIONS OF THE SOUTH, AND ARE FREQUENTLY SERVED WITH CHICKPEAS OR SAUSAGES, AS IN THIS RECIPE.

SERVES FOUR

INGREDIENTS
    50g/2oz/¼ cup butter
    5ml/1 tsp coriander seeds
    225g/8oz green cabbage, shredded
    2 garlic cloves, finely chopped
    50g/2oz cured chorizo sausage,
      roughly chopped
    60ml/4 tbsp dry sherry or white wine
    salt and ground black pepper

VARIATION
Smoked bacon makes a good substitute for chorizo sausage in this recipe, but it should only be cooked briefly.

1 Melt the butter in a frying pan, add the coriander seeds and cook for 1 minute. Add the cabbage to the pan with the garlic and chorizo. Stir-fry for 5 minutes until the cabbage is tender.

2 Add the sherry or wine and plenty of salt and pepper to the pan. Cover and cook for 15–20 minutes until the cabbage is tender. Check the seasoning, adding more if necessary, and serve.

LA CALÇOTADA

Spring onions (calçot) have their own festival in the province of Tarragona. It is a day to mark the return of better weather, and in the past the onions, which were picked when rather bigger than our standard spring onions, were barbecued in the fields.

SERVES SIX

INGREDIENTS
3 bunches of plump spring onions
    (scallions), or Chinese green onions,
    which are about 2.5cm/1in across
    the bulb
olive oil, for brushing
For the romesco sauce
2–3 *ñoras* or other mild dried red
    chillies, such as Mexican
    anchos or *guajillos*
1 large red (bell) pepper, halved
    and seeded
2 large tomatoes, halved and seeded
4–6 large garlic cloves, unpeeled
75–90ml/5–6 tbsp olive oil
25g/1oz/¼ cup hazelnuts, blanched
4 slices French bread, each about
    2cm/¾in thick
15ml/1 tbsp sherry vinegar
squeeze of lemon juice (optional)
chopped fresh parsley, to garnish

1 Prepare the sauce. Soak the dried chillies in hot water for about 30 minutes. Preheat the oven to 220°C/425°F/Gas 7.

2 Place the pepper, tomatoes and garlic on a baking sheet and drizzle with 15ml/1 tbsp olive oil. Roast, uncovered, for 30–40 minutes, until the pepper is blistered and blackened and the garlic is soft. Cool slightly, then peel the pepper, tomatoes and garlic.

COOK'S TIP
This piquant romesco sauce is a variation on the classic, roasting the vegetables rather than frying them.

3 Heat the remaining oil in a small frying pan and fry the hazelnuts until lightly browned, then transfer them to a plate. Fry the bread in the same oil until light brown on both sides, then transfer to the plate with the nuts and leave to cool. Reserve the oil from cooking.

4 Drain the chillies, discard as many of their seeds as you can, then place the chillies in a food processor. Add the red pepper halves, tomatoes, garlic, hazelnuts and bread chunks together with the reserved olive oil. Add the vinegar and process to a paste. Check the seasoning and thin the sauce with a little more oil or lemon juice, if necessary. Set aside.

5 Trim the roots from the spring onions or trim the Chinese onion leaves so that they are about 15–18cm/6–7in long. Brush with oil.

6 Heat an oiled ridged grill pan and cook the onions for about 2 minutes on each side, turning once and brushing with oil. (Alternatively, place under a preheated grill (broiler) 10cm/4in away from the heat and cook for 3 minutes on each side, brushing with more oil when turned; roast in a preheated oven at 200°C/400°F/Gas 6 for 5–6 minutes; or barbecue over grey charcoal for 3–4 minutes on each side, brushing with oil as needed.) Serve immediately with the sauce.

AMANIDA

THE WORD AMANIDA *IS* CATALAN *FOR AN ARRANGED SALAD THAT INCLUDES FISH, MEAT AND VEGETABLES IN EQUAL PROPORTIONS. THESE SALADS CAN BE A WONDER TO BEHOLD, BUT ARE ALSO SIMPLE TO MAKE, BECAUSE THEY COMBINE SMALL QUANTITIES OF READY~TO~EAT INGREDIENTS.*

SERVES SIX

INGREDIENTS
1 lolla green lettuce
50g/2oz cured, sliced chorizo or
  in a piece skinned and diced
4 thin slices Serrano ham
130g/4½oz can sardines
  in oil, drained
130g/4½oz can albacore tuna
  steak in oil, drained
8 canned white asparagus
  spears, drained
2–3 canned palm hearts, drained
115g/4oz/⅔ cup tiny arbequina
  olives
115g/4oz/⅔ cup big gordas or queen
  olives, preferably purplish ones
10 medium red tomatoes
15ml/1 tbsp chopped fresh parsley,
  to garnish
For the vinaigrette
1 garlic clove, split lengthways
30ml/2 tbsp sherry vinegar
30ml/2 tbsp red wine vinegar
60ml/4 tbsp olive oil
60ml/4 tbsp extra virgin olive oil
salt and ground black pepper

COOK'S TIP
The salad selection is largely about what you can get. Fresh asparagus spears (cut to length) can replace canned ones and celery hearts may replace palm heart.

1 Make the vinaigrette. Wipe the cut side of the garlic round a bowl, then discard. Whisk the other ingredients together in the bowl, then tip the vinaigrette into a small jug (pitcher).

2 Choose a large serving plate. Select eight lettuce leaves, to make small bunches round it. Break off the stem ends. Tip the leaves into the vinaigrette bowl and toss to coat in a little dressing. Arrange them around the serving plate.

3 Position the chorizo slices on one side of the plate. Roll the ham and arrange opposite. Drain and blot the canned fish and arrange the sardines and tuna across the plate, in a cross.

4 Arrange the asparagus, spears outwards, and the palm hearts (split lengthways), on opposite sides of the plate. Pile the two types of olive in the remaining spaces.

5 Put the tomatoes in a bowl and pour over boiling water. Leave to stand for 10 minutes, then drain. Peel and quarter two-thirds of the tomatoes and cut out the centres.

6 Arrange the tomatoes, round side up, in the centre of the plate, just touching all the prepared sections. Prepare more tomatoes as they are needed. Arrange them in a flower shape, each new ring just overlapping the previous one. The final ring, in the centre of the pile, should make a flower shape.

7 Brush vinaigrette dressing over the tomatoes, palm hearts and asparagus spears and season lightly with salt and black pepper. Sprinkle parsley very discreetly on the tomatoes and white vegetables. Serve at room temperature. (Refrigerate if you must, while waiting to serve.)

PATATAS BRAVAS

THERE ARE SEVERAL VARIATIONS ON THIS CHILLI AND POTATO DISH, BUT THE MOST IMPORTANT THING IS THE SPICING, WHICH IS MADE HOTTER STILL BY ADDING VINEGAR. THE CLASSIC VERSION IS MADE WITH FRESH TOMATO SAUCE FLAVOURED WITH GARLIC AND CHILLI. THE NAME BRAVAS IMPLIES THAT THE POTATOES ARE SO HOT THAT IT IS MANLY TO EAT THEM.

SERVES FOUR

INGREDIENTS
  675g/1½lb small new potatoes
  75ml/5 tbsp olive oil
  2 garlic cloves, sliced
  3 dried chillies, seeded
    and chopped
  2.5ml/½ tsp ground cumin
  10ml/2 tsp paprika
  30ml/2 tbsp red or white
    wine vinegar
  1 red or green (bell) pepper,
    seeded and sliced
  coarse sea salt, for sprinkling
    (optional)

1 Scrub the potatoes and put them into a pan of salted water. Bring to the boil and cook for 10 minutes, or until almost tender. Drain and leave to cool slightly. Peel, if you like, then cut into chunks.

2 Heat the oil in a large frying or sauté pan and fry the potatoes, turning them frequently, until golden.

3 Meanwhile, crush together the garlic, chillies and cumin using a mortar and pestle. Mix the paste with the paprika and wine vinegar, then add to the potatoes with the sliced pepper and cook, stirring, for 2 minutes. Scatter with salt, if using, and serve hot as a tapas dish or cold as a side dish.

BROAD BEANS WITH BACON

THIS DISH IS PARTICULARLY ASSOCIATED WITH RONDA, IN SOUTHERN SPAIN, THE HOME OF BULL FIGHTING, WHERE BROAD BEANS ARE FED TO FIGHTING BULLS TO BUILD THEM UP. IT IS ALSO FOUND ELSEWHERE IN SPAIN WHERE IT IS KNOWN AS HABAS ESPAÑOLAS. IF YOU HAVE TIME, REMOVE THE DULL SKINS FROM THE BROAD BEANS TO REVEAL THE BRIGHT GREEN BEANS BENEATH.

SERVES FOUR

INGREDIENTS
30ml/2 tbsp olive oil
1 small onion, finely chopped
1 garlic clove, finely chopped
50g/2oz rindless smoked streaky
  (fatty) bacon, roughly chopped
225g/8oz broad (fava) beans, thawed
  if frozen
5ml/1 tsp paprika
15ml/1 tbsp sweet sherry
salt and ground black pepper

VARIATION
For a vegetarian version of this dish use sun-dried tomatoes in oil instead of bacon.

1 Heat the olive oil in a large frying pan or sauté pan. Add the chopped onion, garlic and bacon and fry over a high heat for about 5 minutes, stirring frequently, until the onion is softened and the bacon browned.

2 Add the beans and paprika to the pan and stir-fry for 1 minute. Add the sherry, lower the heat, cover and cook for 5–10 minutes until the beans are tender. Season with salt and pepper to taste and serve hot or warm.

CHILLIES RELLENOS

LARGER CHILLIES ARE OBVIOUSLY EASIER TO STUFF THAN SMALLER ONES. CHORICEROS AND NORAS ARE VERY MILD, BUT YOU CAN USE HOTTER CHILLIES, SUCH AS ANAHEIMS OR POBLANOS IF YOU PREFER OR SUBSTITUTE THE CHILLIES WITH RED PEPPERS.

MAKES SIX

INGREDIENTS
  6 fresh chillies
  2 potatoes, about 400g/14oz
  200g/7oz/scant 1 cup cream cheese
  200g/7oz/1¾ cups grated mature
    (sharp) Cheddar cheese
  5ml/1 tsp salt
  2.5ml/½ tsp ground black pepper
  2 eggs, separated
  115g/4oz/1 cup plain (all-purpose)
    flour
  2.5ml/½ tsp white pepper
  oil, for frying
  chilli flakes to garnish, optional

1 Make a neat slit down one side of each chilli. Place them in a dry frying pan over a moderate heat, turning them frequently until the skins blister.

2 Place the chillies in a strong plastic bag and tie the top to keep the steam in. Set aside for 20 minutes, then carefully peel off the skins and remove the seeds through the slits, keeping the chillies whole. Dry the chillies with kitchen paper and set them aside.

COOK'S TIP
Take care when making the filling; mix gently, trying not to break up the potato pieces.

VARIATION
Whole ancho (dried poblano) chillies can be used instead of fresh chillies, but will have to be reconstituted in water before they can be seeded and stuffed.

3 Scrub or peel the potatoes and cut them into 1cm/½in dice. Bring a large pan of water to the boil, add the potatoes and let the water return to boiling point. Lower the heat and simmer for 5 minutes or until the potatoes are just tender. Do not overcook. Drain them thoroughly.

4 Put the cream cheese in a bowl and stir in the grated cheese, with 2.5ml/ ½ tsp of the salt and the black pepper. Add the potato and mix gently.

5 Spoon some of the potato filling into each chilli. Put them on a plate, cover with clear film and chill for 1 hour so that the filling becomes firm.

6 Put the egg whites in a clean, grease-free bowl and whisk them to firm peaks. In a separate bowl, beat the yolks until pale, then fold in the whites. Scrape the mixture on to a large, shallow dish. Spread out the flour in another shallow dish and season it with the remaining salt and the white pepper.

7 Heat the oil for deep frying to 190ºC/ 375ºF. Coat a few chillies first in flour and then in egg before adding carefully to the hot oil.

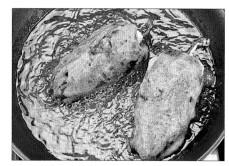

8 Fry the chillies in batches until golden and crisp. Drain on kitchen paper and serve hot, garnished with a sprinkle of chilli flakes for extra heat, if desired.

SWEET TREATS

The Spanish love cakes, biscuits and sweet, sugary snacks. There are an abundance of panaderias (bakeries), heladerias (ice cream parlours) and cake shops in every city and small town. Stands selling churros can be found on many street corners late at night, into the early hours of the morning and at breakfast time.

PANELLETS

The Catalan name for these nutty festival cakes means "little bread", but they are, in fact, much closer to marzipan, with a slightly soft centre that is produced by their secret ingredient – sweet potato. Patisseries make hundreds of these little cakes for All Saints' Day, on 1st November, when families take flowers to the graveyards.

MAKES ABOUT 24

INGREDIENTS
  115g/4oz sweet potato
  butter, for greasing
  1 large (US extra large) egg,
    separated
  225g/8oz/2 cups ground almonds
  200g/7oz/1 cup caster (superfine)
    sugar, plus extra for sprinkling
  finely grated rind of 1 small lemon
  7.5ml/1½ tsp vanilla essence
    (extract)
  60ml/4 tbsp pine nuts
  60ml/4 tbsp pistachio nuts, chopped

1 Dice the sweet potato, and cook it in a pan of boiling water for 15 minutes, or until soft. Drain and leave to cool.

2 Preheat the oven to 200°C/400°F/ Gas 6. Line one or two baking sheets with foil and grease well with butter.

3 Put the cooled sweet potato in a food processor and process to make a smooth purée, then work in the egg yolk, ground almonds, sugar, lemon rind and vanilla essence to make a soft dough. Transfer the dough to a bowl and chill for 30 minutes.

4 Spoon walnut-sized balls of dough on to the foil, spacing them about 2.5cm/ 1in apart, then flatten them out slightly.

5 Lightly beat the egg white and brush over the cakes. Sprinkle half the cakes with pine nuts, slightly less than 5ml/ 1 tsp each, and half with pistachio nuts. Sprinkle lightly with sugar and bake for 10 minutes, or until lightly browned.

6 Leave to cool on the foil, then lift off with a metal spatula.

GUIRLACHE

THIS IS AN ARAB SWEETMEAT FROM THE PYRENEES, COMBINING TOASTED NUTS AND CARAMEL TO PRODUCE A CRISP NUT BRITTLE — A FORERUNNER OF SOME FAMILIAR CHOCOLATE BAR FILLINGS. IT IS LESS WELL KNOWN THAN TURRÓN, THE SPANISH CHRISTMAS NOUGAT, WHICH IS MADE WITH SIMILAR INGREDIENTS AND IS WIDELY AVAILABLE COMMERCIALLY.

MAKES ABOUT 24 PIECES

INGREDIENTS

115g/4oz/1 cup almonds, half
  blanched, half unblanched
115g/4oz/1 cup hazelnuts, half
  blanched, half unblanched
5ml/1 tsp almond oil or
  a flavourless oil
200g/7oz/1 cup granulated sugar
15ml/1 tbsp lemon juice

COOK'S TIP
Guirlache may be served as an after-dinner treat. It is also very good pulverized and used as a topping for mousses and whipped cream. It also makes wonderful ice cream.

1 Preheat the oven to 150°C/300°F/ Gas 2. Scatter the nuts on a baking sheet and toast for about 30 minutes, shaking the sheet occasionally. The nuts should smell pleasant and have turned brown and be very dry.

2 Coarsely chop the toasted nuts or crush them roughly with a rolling pin. Cover another baking tray with foil and grease it generously with the oil.

3 Put the sugar in a pile in a small pan and pour the lemon juice round it. Cook over a high heat, shaking the pan, until the sugar turns a coffee colour. (As it cooks, the pile of sugar will melt and collapse into caramel.)

4 Immediately tip in the nuts and stir once, then pour the mixture on to the foil and spread out into a thin, even layer. Leave the mixture to harden.

5 Once set, break up the caramel into pieces and store in an airtight tin.

PESTIÑOS

THE ARABS INVENTED ALL SORTS OF SWEET BITES, TO EAT AFTER THE MAIN COURSE OR WITH DRINKS. BATHED IN SCENTED HONEY SYRUP, PESTIÑOS WERE OFTEN DEEP-FRIED AND KNOWN AS DULCES DE SÁRTEN, WHICH MEANS "SWEETS FROM THE FRYING PAN". HOWEVER, AT HOME IT IS A GOOD DEAL EASIER TO BAKE THEM AND THEY PUFF BEAUTIFULLY IN THE OVEN.

MAKES ABOUT THIRTY

INGREDIENTS
    225g/8oz/2 cups plain (all-purpose)
        flour, plus extra for dusting
    60ml/4 tbsp sunflower oil
    15ml/1 tbsp aniseed, lightly crushed
    45ml/3 tbsp caster (superfine) sugar
    250ml/8fl oz/1 cup water
    60ml/4 tbsp anisette
    3 small (US medium) eggs
For the anis syrup
    60ml/4 tbsp clear honey
    60ml/4 tbsp anisette

1 Preheat the oven to 190°C/375°F/ Gas 5. Sift the flour on to a sheet of baking parchment. Heat the oil in a small pan with the crushed aniseed, until the aniseed releases its aroma. Strain the oil into a larger pan and add the sugar, water and anisette. Heat to a rolling boil.

2 Remove the pan from the heat and add the sifted flour, all in one go. Beat vigorously with a wooden spoon until the mixture leaves the sides of the pan clean. Leave to cool.

3 Meanwhile lightly beat the eggs. Gradually incorporate the egg into the dough mixture, beating hard. You may not need to use all the egg – the paste should be soft but not sloppy. Reserve any remaining beaten egg.

4 Grease and flour two baking sheets. Fit a plain nozzle to a piping (pastry) bag and pipe small rounds of dough about 2.5cm/1in across on the sheets, spacing them about 2.5cm/1in apart. Brush with the remaining beaten egg.

5 Bake for about 30 minutes, or until lightly brown and an even texture right through. (Lift one off the sheet to test.)

6 Melt the honey in a small pan and stir in the anisette. Just before serving, use a slotted spoon to dunk the *pestiños* into the syrup.

COOK'S TIP
Anisette is a sweet aniseed liqueur that gives the syrup a wonderful flavour. If you cannot find anisette, use another anis spirit such as Ricard instead.

CHURROS

This Spanish breakfast doughnut is sold in all tapas bars, which so conveniently transform into cafés in the morning. Freshly fried, churros accompany a cup of hot chocolate or coffee. They are also served as festival fare, piped into great vats of oil, cut into loops, then tied with grass string and sold to eat while walking along.

MAKES TWELVE TO FIFTEEN

INGREDIENTS
   200g/7oz/1¾ cups plain
     (all-purpose) flour
   1.5ml/¼ tsp salt
   30ml/2 tbsp caster
     (superfine) sugar
   250ml/8fl oz/1 cup water
   60ml/4 tbsp olive or
     sunflower oil
   1 egg, beaten
   caster (superfine) sugar and ground
     cinnamon, for dusting
   oil, for deep-frying

1 Sift the flour, salt and sugar on to a plate or piece of baking parchment. Put the water and oil in a pan and bring to the boil.

2 Tip the flour mixture into the pan and beat with a wooden spoon until the mixture forms a stiff paste. Leave to cool for 2 minutes, then gradually beat in the egg to make a smooth dough.

3 Oil a large baking sheet. Sprinkle plenty of sugar on to a plate and stir in a little cinnamon.

4 Spoon the dough into a large piping (pastry) bag fitted with a 1cm/½in plain piping nozzle. Pipe little coils or "S" shapes on to the baking sheet.

5 Heat 5cm/2in of oil in a large pan to 168°C/336°F, or until a little piece of dough dropped into the oil sizzles on the surface.

6 Using an oiled metal spatula, lower several of the piped shapes into the oil and fry for about 2 minutes until light golden.

7 Drain the churros on kitchen paper, then dip them into the sugar and cinnamon mixture, to coat. Cook the remaining churros in the same way and serve immediately.

TORRIJAS

TRANSLATED AS "POOR KNIGHTS", THESE SUGARED TOASTS ARE PERFECT FOR ALMOST EVERY OCCASION. THEY MAKE A GOOD TEA-TIME SNACK FOR CHILDREN, OR TO ACCOMPANY A CUP OF HOT CHOCOLATE. AS A PARTY DESSERT THEY ARE THE EQUIVALENT OF FRANCE'S TOASTED BRIOCHE — AN ACCOMPANIMENT TO ICE CREAM, OR TO ANY BAKED FRUIT. THEY ARE ALSO VERY POPULAR BY THEMSELVES.

SERVES FOUR

INGREDIENTS
  120ml/4fl oz/½ cup white wine
  2 large (US extra large) eggs
  12 thick rounds of stale
  French bread
  60–90ml/4–6 tbsp sunflower oil
  ground cinnamon, and caster
  (superfine) sugar, for dusting

COOK'S TIP
These toasts are often enjoyed at festivals and are a typical dish from Madrid (although variations can be found all over Europe). Milk can be used in place of white wine, if liked, making them suitable for children.

1 Pour the wine into a shallow dish and dip the bread rounds into it.

2 Beat the eggs together in another shallow dish. Dip half the bread rounds into the beaten egg on each side so that they are completely covered.

3 Heat 60ml/4 tbsp oil in a pan until very hot and fry the bread rounds for about 1 minute on each side until crisp and golden. Reserve on kitchen paper, then dip and fry the rest, adding more oil if necessary. Serve hot, sprinkled with cinnamon and sugar.

SHOPPING INFORMATION

AUSTRALIA

**Anna's Continental
Fine Foods**
3/86 Scarborough Beach Road
Mount Hawthorn
Tel: (08) 9443 1508

Casa Iberica
25 Johnston Street
Fitzroy
Melbourne VIC
Tel: (03) 9419 4420

**Torres Spanish Cellars
& Delicatessen**
75 Liverpool Street
Sydney NSW
Tel: (02) 9264 6862

Viva Spain
315 Victoria Street
Melbourne VIC
Tel: (03) 9329 0485

NEW ZEALAND

**Bel Mondo Italian
Mediterranean Foods**
68 St John
St Tauranga
Tel: (07) 579 0968

Mediterranean Foods Ltd
42 Constable Street
Newtown
Wellington
Tel: (04) 939 8100

UNITED KINGDOM

Bridisa
Borough Market
London SE1
Tel: 020 7403 6932

Casa Pepe
89 High Road
London N2
Tel: 020 8444 9098

Delicioso
Unit 1
Tower Business Park,
Berinsfield
Oxon OX10 7LN
www.delicioso.co.uk

La Coruna
103 Newington Butts
London SE1
Tel: 020 7703 3165

Garcia & Sons
248–250 Portobello Road
London W11
Tel: 020 7221 6119

The Grapevine Delicatessen
77 High Street
Odiham
Hampshire RG29
Tel: 01256 701900

Laymont & Shaw
The Old Chapel
Millpool
Truro
Cornwall TR1
Tel: 01872 270545

Lupe Pinto's Deli
24 Levan Street
Edinburgh EH3
Tel: 0131 228 6241

Maison Bouquillon
41 Moscow Road
London W2
Tel: 020 7229 2107

**Moreno Wine Importers
Co Limited**
11 Marylands Road
London W1
Tel: 020 7286 9678

P de la Fuente
288 Portobello Road
London W10
Tel: 020 7960 5687

Paris and Rios
93 Columbia Road
London E2
Tel: 020 7729 1147

Products from Spain
89 Charlotte Street
London W1
Tel: 020 7580 2905

Rias Altas
97 Frampton Street
London NW8
Tel: 020 7262 4340

UNITED STATES

Dean and Deluca
560 Broadway
New York NY 10012
Tel: (212) 226 6800

Deli Iberico
739 North LaSalle Drive
Chicago IL 60610
Tel: (312) 573 1510

New York Wine Warehouse
8-05 43rd Avenue
Long Island City
New York NY 11101
Tel: (718) 784 8776

Michael Skurnik Wines
575 Underhill Boulevard
Suite 216
Syosset NY 11791
Tel: (516) 677 9300

The Spanish Table
1427 Western Avenue
Seattle WA 98101
Tel: (206) 682 2827
also at:
1814 San Pablo Avenue
Berkley CA 94792
Tel: (510) 548 1383
also at:
109 North Guadalupe Street
Santa Fe NM 87501
Tel: (505) 986 0243

Spectrum Ingredients
5341 Old Redwood Highway
Petaluma CA 94954
Tel: (707) 778 8900

www.chefshop.com
A wide selection of mail order
Spanish ingredients and foods.

www.cmccompany.com
A wide selection of mail order
Spanish ingredients and foods.

www.ethnicgrocer.com
A wide selection of mail order
Spanish ingredients and foods.

www.spanish-gourmet.com
Information about Spanish
ingredients and foods.

PICTURE CREDITS

The publisher would like
to thank the following
photographers and
picture agencies for use
of their images in this
book: Powerstock –
pages 23 (bottom); and
Peter Wilson – pages 22
(top and bottom), and
23 (top).

INDEX